Understanding Power through Watergate

The Washington Collective Power Dynamics

Tian-jia Dong

UNIVERSITY PRESS OF AMERICA,® INC.
Lanham • Boulder • New York • Toronto • Oxford

Copyright © 2005 by
University Press of America,® Inc.
4501 Forbes Boulevard
Suite 200
Lanham, Maryland 20706
UPA Acquisitions Department (301) 459-3366

PO Box 317
Oxford
OX2 9RU, UK

All rights reserved
Printed in the United States of America
British Library Cataloging in Publication Information Available

Library of Congress Control Number: 2005926734
ISBN 0-7618-3153-3 (clothbound : alk. ppr.)
ISBN 0-7618-3154-1 (paperback : alk. ppr.)

∞™ The paper used in this publication meets the minimum
requirements of American National Standard for Information
Sciences—Permanence of Paper for Printed Library Materials,
ANSI Z39.48—1992

This book is dedicated to
my grandparents,
Ma Ke-Xian and Zhu Cui-Zhang,
who nourished my body and
equipped my soul.

Contents

Acknowledgements	vii
Introduction: The Arrogance of Power	1
The Interpersonal Construction of the Presidential Power	1
Nixon and the Republican Party	3
Nixon and Congress	7
The Nixon Way of Dealing with Enemies	10
The Story Line of This Book	11
1 The Interpersonal Power Dynamics Inside Washington	15
The Institutional Role Playing of the FBI and the CIA	15
The Institutional Function of the Justice Department	20
The Patman Investigation	22
The Media and Public Reactions	28
Nixon at the Zenith of His Institutional Power	30
2 The Formation of Washington Collective Power Dynamics	33
The Creation of the Ervin Committee	33
The Immediate Impact	41
The Gray Hearing	44
The Sirica Factor	46
3 The Strength of the Washington Collective Power	50
The Watergate Burglary Trial	50
Breaking McCord	52
The Dean Defection	55
As the Collective Power Dynamics Turned	59

	The "April 30th Explosion" and the Nixon Presidency on Its Deathbed	61
	The Patterned (but Unorganized) Collective Process of Power	64
4	The Difficulty of Genuine Communication in a Mass Society	71
	Reaching-Out: Connecting Washington to the Nation	71
	The Ervin Committee Hearings	75
	The Way Things Were	79
	"Saturday Night Massacre"	84
5	The Difficulty of Uncoupling Inside Washington	90
	The End of the Ervin Committee Hearings	90
	The Tape Transcripts	93
	Power Maneuvering	96
	Further Amassing Collective Power Inside Washington	99
6	The Final Advancement of the Washington Collective Power	105
	Reframing: The Senate Select Committee's Final Report	105
	"Fragile Coalition"	106
	The Supreme Court Ruling on Executive Privilege	109
	The Televised Debate	112
	The Final Advancement	118

Conclusion: Toward a Neo-Progressivism 123
    The Conservative Perspective 123
    The Liberal Perspective 124
    The Radical Left Perspective 125
    The Critical Left Perspective 126
    What Really Worked?—The Social Embeddedness of
        Political Institutions 127
    System Worked, but for Whom—Weapons of the Strong 132
    Toward a Neo-Progressivism 136

Appendix. Methodological Discussions 141
    The Qualitative Method in General 141
    Theory Elaboration Methodology 142
    Issues of Validity and Reliability 144
    The Story-Line Strategy 145
    Sensitizing Concepts 147
    Secondary Data 148
    Open-Ended Research 150

Bibliography 153

Index 159

Acknowledgements

Historical research is usually a lonely job. When I was trying to sort out thousands of data cards filed in my cabinets and striving to make sense of each of them at two o'clock in the morning, I felt a strong sense of solitude. But this research could not in any way be accomplished if I was truly solitary.

First of all, I would like to thank my former teachers. Among them, Professors William Gamson, Diane Vaughan, Paul S. Gray and S. M. Miller at Boston College and Professors Xu Xu-dian, Pan Qun and Wang Wen-quan at Shandong University deserve the most gratitude. They were the most knowledgeable and responsible teachers I have ever known. They transformed my life by teaching me knowledge and, more significantly, by touching me with scholarly decency and humanity.

Professor Andrew Walder invited me to Harvard University as a visiting scholar in 1991. That position provided me with a precious opportunity to take root in an American academic environment. I would like to thank him with a grateful heart.

I am deeply indebted to Professors William Harris and Frank Soo at Boston College. They are my teachers and my friends. I deeply grateful for their teacherly guidance and friendly help during and after my Boston College years.

I would also like to express my deep gratitude to Dr. Janet Surrey and Dr. Steve Bergman, as well as their lovely daughter, Katie. They have been my best friends since the first year I started my American journey and have helped me in countless ways throughout these years.

My colleagues at Westfield State College deserve special gratitude. Dr. Kate Bagley, Dr. Zengie Mangoliso, Dr. Robert Kersting, Dr. Jane Mildred, and Ms. Nancy Boistelle provided me with a warm and supportive environment. It was only because of this environment that I could have a peaceful mind to concentrate on my research.

I would like to thank Ms. MacDuff Stewart and Ms. Beverly Baum at University Press of America. This book would not have become a reality without their enthusiasm and professionalism.

Every time I accomplish something, I like to think about my family. Since I grew up in my grandparents' house, I have a big family to think about and thank. My parents, Dong Zhen-lin and Ma Xiao-ji, experienced so much material and emotional hardship to support me. My father passed away in 1999. The emotional loss inside me still persists. My aunts and my uncles also surrounded me with love and care. My two sisters, Dr. Hui-jia Dong and Dr. Yi-jia Dong have been so selfless to me that they always think about me first before they take care of themselves. I thank them and my two brothers-in-law, Dr. Chen Liu and Dr. Gong-chao Wang, and my nieces and nephew, Joy, David and Qian-qian. My eight cousins and I grew up together in my grandparents' house, and they have been my strong supporters throughout these years. My emotional connection to all of them is eternal.

This book is dedicated to my grandparents. My grandfather, a learned historian and dedicated teacher, taught me the basic things, like how to draw the first picture, how to recognize the first Chinese character, and how to recite the first classic Chinese poem, to the most complicated theories, like how to understand human society. He taught me what a meaningful individual life should be and what an ideal society should be. I can never forget the times when he held a very thick classic history book to teach me about the calendar and agricultural production in ancient China, wars and uprisings, changes in the imperial courts, and all the other important things about how traditional Chinese society worked. His scholarly decency, his breadth of vision and mind, transformed me fundamentally.

My grandmother, a house wife for all her life, provided me with rich food to eat, warm clothing to wear, and plenty of advice that eventually shaped me into a useful member of society. In the periods of time after the Great Famine (from 1959 through 1962) and during the Cultural Revolution, it was a hugely difficult job to feed everybody in the family. To be able to avoid starving was already difficult enough. But my grandmother endured extra hardship to go beyond that. She struggled to get me 12 oz of milk each day and an egg twice a week—very few children could enjoy such a "luxury" at that time. In situations in which preparing every meal was a struggle, my grandmother always found ways to make every meal delicious and nutritious. She also made almost all of my clothing, as well as my shoes. In my memory, my grandmother never sat there relaxing. She was always busy with something. She always got up at 5:30 in the morning and worked without stopping until all of us went to sleep after 9:30 at night. Both of my grandparents passed away more than ten years ago, but their spirit will be with me always.

My wife, Dr. Dongxiao Qin, has been enthusiastically supporting me throughout the long and challenging journey of research and writing. As a feminist, she is relational and independent. She tried her best to free me from many house-hold duties and thus enabled me to concentrate on this research. As an accomplished psychologist, she offered me insightful ideas that have challenged me and sharpened my thoughts. More importantly, as an "old couple" married for more than eighteen years, we experienced a mutually supportive and mutually stimulating spiritual growth. Our most constant daily conversations are our reflections and thoughts about the divine power of social justice and equality. I have been motivated and inspired by our common spiritual pursuit throughout the struggles of my life.

My son, Daniel Zai, was born after I just started this research. He has been the most powerful inspiration from the very beginning. As the research was slowly progressing, he has become a little boy who can argue with me about some social issues. He has been the sunshine in my dark times; he has been the timely rain when my energy and motivation dried out. He is the hope of my future; the happiness of his generation is the sole purpose of this book.

Tian-jia Dong
November 30th, 2004

Introduction: The Arrogance of Power

INTERPERSONAL CONSTRUCTION OF THE PRESIDENTIAL POWER

The presidential power seemed enormous to those working in the executive branch of the government. The Nixon presidency marked a further evolution of a managerial style, which presented a presidency like a monarchical court. Former Johnson aide George Reedy accurately portrayed White House life. He observed that the entire White House was designed to serve the material needs of the President, from providing the most luxurious means of travel to having a masseur constantly present. The President was treated with kingly reverence. "No one speaks to him unless spoken to first. No one ever invites him to 'go soak your head' when his demands become petulant and unreasonable."[1] Nixon was also a master of micro-management. He had a strong drive for personal control and liked to be intensely involved in routine operations, including those most petty.

How was the power of the Nixon presidency organized? On the surface, the presidential power seemed rational, formal, and orderly. It was an institution with clear rules and distinctive role assignments. However, all the facts revealed demonstrated that the power organization of the Nixon presidency was neither rationally nor formally routinized. It was a mixture of personal ties and utilitarian bindings. The only rule people followed was to serve and make connections with the more powerful power holders in order to build personal connections with them and then to show off to others. John Dean described the typical internal dynamic of the power process in the Nixon presidency:

> For a thousand days I would serve as counsel to the President. I soon learned that to make my way upward, into a position of confidence and influence, I had

to travel downward through factional power plays, corruption and finally outright crimes. Although I would be rewarded for diligence, true advancement would come from doing those things which built a common bond of trust—or guilt—between me and my superiors. In the Nixon White House, these upward and downward paths diverged, yet joined, like prongs of a tuning fork pitched to a note of expediency. Slowly, steadily, I would climb toward the moral abyss of the President's inner circle until I finally fell into it, thinking I had made it to the top just as I began to realize I had actually touched bottom.[2]

Such informal, irrational, but routinized internal power dynamics would inevitably develop and externalize into an "arrogance of power." In the 1960s, it was not uncommon for the government to wiretap political opposition in the anti-war and civil right movements. Since this was a struggle between "we" and "they", the insider and the outsider, nobody in the high circles of the political system had the slightest desire to expose such an illegal program. Most of them were wholehearted supporters of it. Then, the targets of aggressive wiretapping expanded to include reporters and suspected disloyalists in the government. Since the victims were scattered and weak, weak enough to not be able to launch any defensive and offensive actions, these illegal activities were simply sustained and expanded. The arrogance of power was thus maintained. It was only natural to expand this convenient tool to deal with insiders of the system when internal power struggle became intensified, especially during an election year. A typical performance of the power play was that the stronger side of power always ignored the weaker side. They always assumed they had the power to hold on to the current power structure, therefore, they could put the weak side in a disadvantaged position and mistreat them at will.

The break-in on June 17, 1972, of the Democratic headquarters by four Cuban Americans and James McCord, security coordinator for the Committee for the Re-Election of the President, was organized under the direction of the CREEP General Counsel G. Gordon Liddy and his partner both at the CREEP and at the Plumber's unit in the White House, Howard Hunt. This was a natural extension of the Nixon Administration's power game. However, the break-in seemed like a big surprise to all citizens, even highly powered, organized citizens. As an elite journalist, Elizabeth Drew found it hard to make sense of it. She described the typical mentality: "When we heard about that break-in on a weekend in June, it seemed odd—we didn't know what to make of it—and it was hard to decide what to think."[3]

The behavior of this "arrogance of power" continued even after the arrest of five Watergate burglars. White House spokesperson Ronald L. Ziegler only briefly answered a question about the break-in at the Watergate by describing the incident as "a third-rate burglary attempt" not worthy of further White House comment.

Throughout the period after June 17, 1972 to the end of 1972, the White House's campaign to contain the investigation can be characterized as, using a favorite word of Nixon: "stone-walling."

According to Dean, the man who was in charge of the implementation of this strategy, the "stonewall" was ad hoc, developed in small reactions to the daily events. There was no overall and systematic plan for the cover-up.[4] How did the President's men implement such an ad hoc "stone-walling"? It was a series of reactions and adjustments to ever changing power dynamics.

NIXON AND THE REPUBLICAN PARTY

Sidney Milkis describes the relationship between presidents and political parties in general:

> The relationship between the presidency and the American party system has always been difficult. The architects of the Constitution established a nonpartisan president who, with the support of the judiciary, was intended to play the leading institutional role in checking and controlling the 'violence of faction' that the framers feared would rend the fabric of representative democracy. Even after the presidency became a more partisan office during the early part of the nineteenth century, its authority continued to depend on an ability to transcend party politics. The president is nominated by a party but, unlike the British prime minister, is not elected by it."[5]

Since Roosevelt, the role of the Democratic Party and the Republican Party alike had become preempted in many significant fields following the institutionalization of the developing and expanding administrative presidency. The traditional duties of the two parties, which were diminishing, included providing a link from government to interest groups, staffing the executive department, contributing to policy development, and organizing election campaigns. This trend had been developing well into the Johnson administration. The rupture between the presidency and the party made it difficult to sustain political enthusiasm and organizational support for the Great Society. After the Democrats' poor showing in the 1966 congressional election, many Democrats strongly criticized Johnson's inattention to party politics, criticism that continued until Johnson withdrew from the presidential campaign in 1968. As James Rowe, who was Johnson's campaign director in both 1964 and 1968, complained at one point to Johnson's personnel director Macy by saying, "Perhaps you can train some of those career men to run the political campaigns in 1968. (It ain't as easy as you government people appear to think it is.)"[6]

The relationship between the president and his own party in the Nixon presidency was a natural extension of the practices from Roosevelt through Johnson. However, it was more dramatic in the Nixon administration in the centralization of authority in the White House and the reduction of regular Republican organization to perfunctory status. In this way, Nixon lost one crucial battle in enhancing his position in the power dynamics. He did not only lose the crucial support from his own party, but also lost the opportunities to nurture close interpersonal ties between himself and those powerful Republican politicians.

In late 1971, Nixon created another personalized organization, the Committee to Re-Elect the President (CREEP), which raised money and otherwise operated entirely independently from the Republican Party and the Republican National Committee (RNC). The complete autonomy of the Committee for the Re-Election of the President from the Republican National Committee in the 1972 campaign was but the final stage of a long process of White House preemption of the RNC's political responsibilities. In the campaign, Nixon self-indulgently sought to beat Lyndon Johnson's 1964 margins and strove for winning all the states. Therefore, the Nixon campaign focused on the presidential race and made little effort to create any coattail effect for lesser Republicans. Nixon failed to capture any working majority in Congress. The Democrats gained two seats in the Senate and lost twelve in the House and therefore remained in control of Congress by margins of 57-43 in the Senate and 243-192 in the House.

The fact was that Nixon willingly sidestepped giving support to Republican candidates. He told Ehrlichman, Mitchell, and Magruder, a year earlier before the congressional campaign began, that Democrats who had opposed the Mansfield Amendment for a cutoff in support for the Vietnam War would not face "significant" Republican opposition. Personally, Nixon spoke bitterly of his party. He declared that in 1970 "I broke my ass for the party at considerable cost." To many fellow Republicans, this kind of action revealed Nixon's mean and self-important mentality, which discouraged many being associated with him. Even worse than his unwillingness to contribute to the enlargement and strengthening of Republican group power as a whole, Nixon even thought of reducing the power of the Republican National Committee and simply folding it into the White House. He told Ehrlichman that he had never stood higher in public esteem, while the Republican National Committee had never stood lower.[7]

The conservative force in the Republican Party was the pillar of the Nixon administration from its very beginning and Senator Berry Goldwater was a key figure in the conservative camp. On the Nixon side, the policy maneuvers brought Nixon and his conservative allies together. He also made some efforts to make the personal relationship between himself and Goldwater closer. Nixon did not want to alienate Goldwater because he carried weight with conservatives, and he needed his support.[8]

But, in fact, the relationship between Nixon and those major powerful figures in the conservative camp was more like a love-and-hate affair. As Robert Alan Goldberg recorded, as early as the beginning of the Nixon administration, Goldwater had some doubt about and frustration with Nixon. He wanted to secure patronage and an appointment that he needed badly because of his political IOUs, but he failed. Also, Goldwater had trouble scheduling an appointment to meet Nixon. "After repeated attempts, he finally visited with the president in early March 1969. He would not confer again with the president in private for six months, and after that not until December 1970. Clearly there was substance to his grievance: he was 'never consulted about political matters.'"[9]

In his 1988 memoir, Goldwater described his impression of Nixon: "He was the most dishonest individual I ever met in my life."[10] "Nixon seemed outwardly friendly but inwardly remote."[11]

As to the relationship between himself, the other leaders of the conservative camp, and Nixon, Goldwater wrote of two major incidents. First was a scenario reflecting the relationship between Nixon and another conservative leader, Reagan, then California Governor. After Nixon's first inauguration, Reagan was host at a ball in the Sheraton Hotel. But when Nixon arrived, he was not introduced to the crowd by Reagan, the host. Instead, he was introduced by TV host Art Linkletter. This would have been strange in Washington. To Berry Goldwater, "some signals had been crossed." More significantly, after his remarks, Nixon walked directly past the box of Reagan and his wife, Nancy, without shaking hands or saying hello. As Goldwater observed: "I was then certain there had been no mix-up. It was deliberate."[12]

Another scenario was about himself and Nixon:

> On February 15, 1969, about six weeks after Nixon entered the Oval Office, I added to my private file, "I've tried for three days to get an appointment with President Nixon. I'm beginning to be afraid that a wall has been built around him. Nixon has told me on quite a few occasions that, if I wanted anything from him, all I had to do was ask.[13]

Political parties in the U.S. are essentially interpersonal networks. Without a solid interpersonal power base in his own party, Nixon's support among those powerful politicians was greatly weakened. As Milkis described: "The evolution of the modern presidency now left the office in complete institutional isolation."[14] The Nixon presidency was institutionally more isolated. However, more significantly, Nixon, as one of those powerful politicians, was even more isolated from the interpersonal connections with his peers.

This point can be made clearer by looking at the relationship between Reagan and the Republican Party. Reagan broke with the tradition of the modern presidency. He identified closely with his party and maintained close ties with those powerful in the party. He, on behalf of those party powerfuls, made enormous efforts to strengthen the Republicans' organizational and popular base. By his "total readiness" to shoulder such partisan responsibilities as making numerous fund-raising appearances for the party and its candidates, Reagan brought the enthusiasm of a convert to Republican activities and strengthened the interconnected inter-party personal connections. A stronger interpersonal network brought a stronger party as a whole. The stronger Republican group power, in turn, provided stronger and richer resources for Reagan to mobilize in his political battle.

Reagan greatly benefited from the strong relationship between himself and the interpersonal networks in the Republican Party. The Republican Party's strength solidified Reagan's personal popularity and facilitated the support of his program in Congress, and, especially, the strong interpersonal networks brought him the support of a formidable institution when he was in trouble during the Iran-Contra affair. The Reagan presidency, like other presidencies, also pursued its program with acts of administrative discretion that short-circuited the legislative process and weakened efforts to carry out broadly based party policies. But the Iran-Contra scandal would be a very serious violation, much more serious and more damaging to the system than most of the violations of its kind. However, it was regarded by those powerful politicians in the Republican Party as rather uncharacteristic and exceptional, as Senator Richard Lugar of Indiana, who as the Chair of the Foreign Relations Committee from 1985 to 1987, acted as Reagan's Senate floor leader in matters of foreign policy, had said. Lugar considered the Iran-Contra affair to have been a "glaring exception" to Reagan's general willingness to consult with Congress and to work closely with Republican leadership. The Iran-Contra affair would be a rather "uncharacteristic inattention to partisan responsibility."[15] The underlining meaning was clear: as long as you are willing to share power interpersonally, your damage to the state system will be excused. Reagan thus got enormous support from the Republican Party which helped him get away with the serious violation of law in the Iran-Contra affair. At many critical junctures in the investigation, it was Republican leaders in the Congress, like Bob Dole, and Republican loyalists in the judiciary system, like Judges Laurence Silberman and David Bryan Sentelle, who protected and defended Reagan.

The Clinton-Monica affair also demonstrated the importance of the informal interpersonal relationship between a president and the powerful of his own party. Clinton had a luke-warm relationship with those powerful politicians in the Democratic Party. He appeared indifferent to their programmatic commitments and election prospects. At the beginning of the affair, few Democrats came to the president's defense. In fact, as the New York Times reported, "It is the people who know [Clinton] best—from his own former aides to his wary fellow Democrats in Congress—who have been most disappointed and angry about his handling of the Monica Lewinsky matter, and who have held it against him more harshly than a detached and distant public."[16] A personal scandal therefore mushroomed into a huge political incident. It was clear that although Clinton may have had allies in his party, he had few close friends. During the impeachment process, Clinton luckily got strong support from most Democrats, who saved his presidency. But they fought, not for him, but for their disdain for the Republican majority.

NIXON AND CONGRESS

The Constitution says that Congress should make the laws and that the President should "take care that the laws be faithfully executed." The power of government was designed by the Framers to be separated between Congress, the President and the Supreme Court. However, in practice, power is in essence inseparable. If a person is powerful enough, he will be powerful everywhere on every issue with which he concerns himself. Whether he is powerful or not, to a large extent, depends on whether he can network other powerful people and become the center of them. Power follows powerful people. The institutional construction of separation of powers works only to the extent that a fair number of people, rather than one person or few people, gain the power to dominate. Power is therefore not an institutionally assigned, rigidly constructed objective "thing." It is formed and developed in the process of social dynamics. Here lies the true nature of the institutional separation of powers into checks and balances.

The situation, in reality, would instead be that power is not separated institutionally but shared by those powerful politicians as individuals in a form of interpersonal connections. Power dynamics exist in a social process that enables individuals to share power. Whether separation of powers is reality or not depends on whether power is socially shared or not. That is to say, each powerful individual is a center of a network and how powerful he is depends on how large the network is. The size of networks enables him to have power over other individuals in other branches. Therefore, the Constitutional checks and balances are not based upon the Constitutional arrangement that separates powers between the three government branches. Such an institutional buildup is just an organizational form. As Neustadt insightfully pointed out, the checks and balances are embedded in the sharing of one power among many powerful individuals, not a separating of powers, among those government branches.[17] Because of the struggle for the lion's share of government power, those powerful politicians have been checking on each other and thus have relatively balanced the power operation.

From the network perspective, the sheer number of congressmen/women and senators—538 of them—in Congress would make it as an institutional whole perform badly. In fact, it is difficult for Congress to conduct collective work simply because of its numbers. So many people, each with his/her own big ego, make Congress essentially a reactive branch. In most cases it simply neglects its institutional duties. For instance, Congress is institutionally supposed to initiate law and establish legislation, but fewer and fewer enterprises are initiated by Congress. Increasingly the laws are written in the executive branch, then passed, perhaps in revised form, by Congress. Also, Congress is supposed to watch the executive branch to see how the laws are carried out by the executive, how the office of the President is executed, or whether the Constitution is being preserved. However, Congress often pays little attention to these matters. It would not be easy to mobilize either house of Congress to act actively and coherently.

However, as Morris Fiorina asserted: "Whatever animated by a selfish urge to do well or a generous desire to do good, the modern member of Congress wants to be reelected."[18] Richard Fenno explained, "For most members of Congress most of the time, [the] electoral goal is primary. It is the prerequisite for a congressional career and, hence, for the pursuit of other member goals."[19] Therefore, although Congress's main constitutional task is to legislate in the national interest, most of the activities that produce votes for members are nonlegislative, primarily "pork-barreling" and casework. Pork-barreling involves getting federal grant and project money for their home states and districts; casework is handling constituents' complaints about their personal experiences with the federal bureaucracy.[20]

Therefore, political leaders on Capitol Hill work more like individuals and less like institutional functionaries. As individuals, they share the executive power with the President. They perform this kind of interpersonal power much more effectively than they perform their formal institutional duties. For instance, powerful Senators or House members usually recommend their close associates to the President for positions, some of them important ones, in the executive branch. Whether these recommendations can be accommodated really depends on the power dynamics. If those powerful senators or House members are powerful enough in the eyes of the President, the invisible hand of power will fill the position with those who have connections with the members of Congress. On the other hand, if the President does not see the politicians in Congress who ask for these favors as powerful enough, he will be able to afford to ignore their recommendations. In the latter case, the congressional power of sharing personnel appointments will be reduced.

Nixon's offense to other powerful politicians was not because his aggressive expansion of his power violated the legal and formal separation of powers between government branches, but because he refused to share power based on the existing and informal power structure among powerful political leaders in Washington. He attempted to reduce those powerful politicians' power which they had enjoyed all along. In this way he went far beyond the limitation of the socially constructed power dynamics. His power therefore became a spent force. As he went forward, more and more powerful people signed up as his enemies. In the end, the resistance became so strong that Nixon's institutional power eventually became an arrow at the end of its flight.

From the start, Nixon and his close associates followed the path he had laid out in a 1968 campaign talk: to create the magic working relationship of the President and the People and so make Congress irrelevant. Nixon sought to bypass Congress to forge an alliance between himself and the New American Majority—his new label for the hitherto Silent Majority. The confrontation was between the President—elected as he was by over 60 percent of those voting—and the New Minority. This New Minority represented unlikable special interests—such as Senator Edward Kennedy on labor policies; Senator William Proxmire on banking affairs; Senator J. William Fulbright and Frank Church on international relations and defense policies.[21] However, as a guilty man with so many criminal actions under his name, Nixon failed to secure sustained support from most powerful politicians in Congress. He was over confidant about his institutional power over the "Silent Majority" and overlooked the informally and socially constructed interpersonal power among those powerful politicians.

The aggressive power expansion by the Nixon White House decreased Congressional influence over the Cabinet and all other agencies in the executive branch. Members of Congress thus potentially lost much of their traditional power in dealing with caseworks, because their rate of success depended upon their influence on federal agencies. Many powerful politicians felt the impact. While this power struggle was invisible to most voters, it was the key item in Washington as Nixon's second term began.

The power concentration and centralization in the second Nixon administration was far clearer than the first one. Even the traditional powers of cabinet officers were reduced and moved to the White House. In the White House, there formed a layer of "super-Cabinet officers" like Henry Kissinger and John Ehlichman, who coordinated policy, pushed the bureaucratic work and prevented bureaucratic delay. They started a trend that more and more executive branch operations were handled by and for the White House. The problem for this transformation was that it broke the connections that had traditionally existed among the president and those powerful politicians who had their own power base. By alienating those cabinet officers, Nixon lost these men's power base, while their power base could be mobilized in support of the presidential needs. More significantly, none of these transformations received congressional approval. That is to say, none of the benefit developed from these moves would be shared by powerful political leaders in Congress. They were even deprived of some of their traditional power. The most sensitive issue was that the new layer of "super-Cabinet officers" or their superior, White House Chief of Staff Haldeman, would not be accountable to Congress. The White House was trying to create a new type of executive branch controlled by those whose total loyalty was to Richard Nixon.[22]

Nixon further challenged the members of Congress right on the pocketbook issue—he announced that he would "impound" congressional appropriations. "Impoundment" meant that if the legislators funded programs the President disapproved of, or voted more funds for something than he thought sufficient, he would veto the bills. Then, if Congress passed the bills over his veto, the President would still refuse to spend the money. In this way, the congressional power to distribute federal funds would be greatly reduced and those members of Congress would sharply feel the loss of power when they tried to use the kinds of "pork-barreling" power for their political gains. Depending upon their specific political needs, some members wanted money for pork barrels, others for social-welfare programs, and everybody needed something from subsidies to agriculture to the funding of certain regulatory agencies. Nixon thus became such a threat that many powerful politicians started to unite. Also, the timing was bad for Nixon. His announcement of impoundment was right on the eve of the Gray-McCord-Sirica shocks; political temperatures on Capitol Hill therefore rose.[23]

THE NIXON WAY OF DEALING WITH ENEMIES

Nixon not only had many "natural" enemies among powerful politicians because of policy differences or ideology, he also created many more personal ones. They were composed of, as Nixon himself termed it, the "Washington iron triangle"—legislators, bureaucracy, and lobbyists, plus the media. The powerful politicians in Congress were the most powerful ones who had the final power to smash Nixon's aggressive expansion of power.

The most extreme example of what Nixon had done, most threatening to his enemies in particular and to all powerful people in general, was the creation of the Special Investigative Unit, more familiarly known as the "Plumbers." This organization was responsible only to the President's personal direction. It was a sign of power for power's sake. The White House view of its "enemies" eventually expanded to include not only antiwar activists but also those who operated within the traditional framework of political conflict. Plumbers were used in the fight to bypass the usual channels to implement illegal operations.

At the same time, Nixon's subordinates abused the presidential power even further. In August 1971, White House Counsel John Dean started preparing the "enemies list" at the request of Haldeman and Ehrlichman. The idea of the enemies' list was to "maximize the fact of our incumbency in dealing with persons known to be more active in their opposition to our Administration." This involved the use of "the available federal machinery to screw our political enemies."[24] Within a month, Charles Colson provided a modest list of twenty names. Senator Edmund Muskie's chief fundraiser and the AFL-CIO's political director headed the list. The number quickly grew to over two hundred as others in the Administration chimed in with their favorite enemies, including institutions as well as individuals. Included were obvious political opponents, such as Kennedy, Muskie, and Senator Walter Mondale. Haldeman selected a number of people on the various lists for IRS audits and other forms of harassment. Nixon later candidly acknowledged his own involvement in such harassment. He "hit the ceiling," he recalled, when he learned that the IRS had audited John Wayne and Billy Graham. He told his aides: "Get the word out, down to IRS, that I want them to conduct field audits of those who are our opponents, if they're going to do in our friends." He immediately suggested Democratic National Chairman Larry O'Brien as a target.[25]

By aggressively expanding his own power and relentlessly reducing other powerful politicians' power, Nixon actively grew offensive to those powerful politicians and many other powerful people in the political establishment. Nixon, after winning a landslide victory, was about to suffer the consequences of the arrogance of power he had constructed over his years as President of the United States. Nixon's abuse of his victory in the election paved the way for his defeat. Once a collective power dynamics formed in the circle among Washington political leaders, a drama began.

THE STORY LINE OF THIS BOOK

The Watergate affair is officially regarded as a case of break-in, of cover-up, and of abuse of power by the Nixon Administration. It is considered, in a popular myth, to be an instance of a political deviance in the framework of the American political system, which included such violations as bribery, perjury, obstruction of justice, forgery, burglary, and abuse of government power to repress political opponents, to list some of the most frequently mentioned.

The popular myth about the reaction of the American political system to this scandal is reflected in two television documentaries, which are twenty-four years apart, although their story line remains the same. The first documentary is "The Scandal That Was Watergate," first broadcast in December 1979 on CBS. The second is "Watergate—plus 30: shadow of history," broadcast in 2003 on PBS. The hidden drama is described along a clear story line: how the underground river of illegal actions was brought to the light, how the good guys backed by the legal system defeated the bad guys who were trying to damage the system—among the bad guys were the President and his associates. The story started with how powerful the bad guys were—how the President and his associates had used the great power of his office, first to control and limit the investigation of the break-in and then to prevent the tapes from becoming public and being used as evidence. But eventually, the courts, together with Congress, backed by public opinion, finally forced the release of the tapes and produced the "smoking pistol that would shoot Nixon down." Thirty years after the scandal, after deep reflections and soul-searching, this one sentence still stands: "Our constitution worked." Most of the textbooks to educate future generations about the nature of Watergate adopted this story line, that is, "the system worked," "democracy had prevailed," or "the rule of law had been vindicated."

This depiction is closely related to the classic pluralist assumptions about the American political system. It assumes that the political institutions symbolized by the Constitution would guarantee the following: (1) an "open field" competition of social groups; (2) a functional role in society at large as the source of political power; (3) the individual pursuit of collective goal as the roots of authority; (4) the pluralist nature of government as the instrument of authority. The formal and institutionalized state construction enables that the system works effectively and all deviations and corruptions are dealt with timely; and in the end, no one, or interest, will become dominant.

Underneath this popular myth, four perspectives can be identified in the ocean of discussions about Watergate. The first two perspectives focus on the Nixon Administration's violations—how their behaviors violated the law and public trust and how the public and its representatives in Congress and the law enforcement branch in the government exposed those violations and reacted accordingly. The conservative perspective and the liberal perspective share this same view. The difference between them is whether the system worked automatically or it worked only by accident. Ironically, the ultra-right and the leftist views share a same point of departure. Both of them focus on the social construction of Watergate scandal. They regard Watergate as a product of making through power dynamics—discovery and outrage were socially made by certain powerful groups. The difference is that, for the ultra-right, it was the liberals to get Nixon; for the leftists, it was the men of power or the state system as a whole to maintain the power structure of the status quo.

This research differs from all of these four perspectives. It focuses on the issue of the social embeddedness of political institutions. It does not enthrone the formal state institutions but centers on the Washington collective power dynamics. The aftermath of the Watergate break-in is treated as a good example to highlight these underlying mechanisms of the political system. The research therefore reveals and analyzes four major stages that constituted the entire Watergate investigation and presidential impeachment process. The first stage began with the break-in on June 17, 1972, and went through Nixon's overwhelming re-election and its immediate aftermath. Nixon's "arrogance of power" which was reflected by the interpersonal power dynamics dominated this stage. The second stage was driven by the effective interpersonal networking efforts of Senators Mansfield and Ervin, which shaped a powerful collective power dynamics among Washington political leaders. It started with the New Year of 1973, lasting through the "April Explosion," and ended in May, when the Nixon presidency was put on its deathbed. The third stage was one of agenda-framing in the public domain, which consisted of the Ervin Committee Hearings and other events through the "Saturday Night Massacre". This stage would be characterized by the superficial connection between the Washington political leaders and citizens in general. The forth stage was shaped by the efforts of uncoupling between the Washington political leaders and Nixon. It included all maneuvers driven by the Washington collective power dynamics from October 1973 to August 8, 1974, when Nixon resigned from the Presidency.

NOTES

1. Reedy, George. *The Twilight of the Presidency.* (New York: The World Publishing Co.: 1970), 18.

2. Dean, John W. III. *Blind Ambition: The White House Years.* (New York: Simon & Shuster, 1976), 30–31.

3. Drew, Elizabeth. Washington Journal: the events of 1973–1974. (New York: Random House: 1975), 15.

4. Dean, *Blind Ambition,* 121.

5. Milkis, Sidney. "The Presidency and Political Parties." in Nelson, Michael (ed.) *The Presidency and the Political System (sixth ed.).* (Washington, D. C.: CQ Press, 2000), 376.
6. Milkis, Sidney. "The Presidency and Political Parties." In Nelson, 384–385.
7. Kutler, Stanley I. *The Wars of Watergate: The Last Crisis of Richard Nixon.* (New York: Knopf, 1990), 237–238.
8. Goldberg, Robert Alan. *Barry Goldwater.* (New Haven, CT.: Yale University Press, 1995), 258.
9. Goldberg, *Barry Goldwater,* 257–258.
10. Goldwater, Barry M. and Jack Casserly. *Goldwater.* (New York: Doubleday, 1988), 255.
11. Goldwater and Casserly. *Goldwater,* 256.
12. Goldwater and Casserly. *Goldwater,* 256.
13. Goldwater and Casserly. *Goldwater,* 257.
14. Milkis, Sidney. "The Presidency and Political Parties." in Nelson, 388
15. Milkis, Sidney. "The Presidency and Political Parties." in Nelson, 388
16. New York Times, Sept. 17, 1998: 18
17. Neustadt, Richard E. *Presidential Power—the politics of leadership from FDR to Carter.* (New York: Macmillan Publishing Company, 1980), 26.
18. Fiorina, Morris. *Congress: Keystone of the Washington Establishment.* 2nd ed. (New Haven, CT.; Yale University Press, 1989), 37.
19. Fenno, Richard Jr. *Home Style: House Members in Their Districts.* (Boston: Little, Brown, 1978), 31.
20. Fiorina, *Congress,* 41–49.
21. Kutler, *The Wars of Watergate,* 127; 245.
22. McQuaid, Kim. Morrow, *The Anxious Years—America in the Vietnam-Watergate era.* (New York: Basic Books, 1989), 221; Sundquist, James L. *The Decline and Resurgence of Congress.* (Washington D.C.: Brookings Institution, 1981), 1–4; 210–215.
23. McQuaid, *The Anxious Years,* 221; Sundquist, *The Decline and Resurgence of Congress,* 210–215; Schell, Jonathan. *The Time of Illusion: An Historical and Reflective Account of the Vietnam Era.* (New York: Vintage Books, 1976), 309–311.
24. Dean, *Blind Ambition,* 316.
25. Lukas, Anthony J. *Nightmare: The Underside of the Nixon Years.* (New York: Viking Press, 1976), 12–18; U.S. Congress, Senate, Select Committee. *The Final Report of the Select Committee on Presidential Campaign Activities.* (Washington, D.C.: U.S. Government Printing Office, June 1974), 135–143.

Chapter One

The Interpersonal Power Dynamics Inside Washington

THE INSTITUTIONAL ROLE PLAYING OF THE FBI AND THE CIA

Career civil servants in general, who represent virtually 99 percent of the federal workforce, are motivated by, wrote Erwin Hargrove, "their career, agency, and program. The markers of success are autonomy for their bureaus and expansion of budgets." Such self-interested commitments make life difficult for the remaining few: the departmental secretaries, undersecretaries, assistant secretaries, and other political executives whom the president appoints to manage the bureaucracy in pursuit of the administration's policy.[1] This is a rather popular view of the federal bureaucracy. However, the conduct of the Nixon administration changed this stereotype. Richard Cole and David Caputo conducted a survey about the bureaucracy under the Nixon administration. They discovered that most super-grade bureaucrats, including Democrats and especially independents, by then supported Nixon's policies. "We find the 'pull' of the presidency to be very strong," Cole and Caputo concluded. A plausible explanation would be that informal power dynamics used by Nixon produced the harmony of self-interest between career bureaucrats and a strong president. Cole and Caputo reported that the Nixon administration played an unusually purposeful and active role in building the interpersonal power dynamics between the administration and the career officials through the job-promotion process within the upper reaches of the civil service. "Loyal" civil servants were favored. This group included Republicans, of course, but also many independents and some Democrats who recognized that the administration meant business and therefore adapted this kind of power dynamics in order to further their own careers.[2] Here, informal and active interpersonal power dynamics made impact.

The FBI assumed primary responsibility for the investigation of the Watergate break-in. The first stage of the FBI investigation and the U.S. Attorney's handling of the case before the New Year of 1973 were later criticized as inept, unnecessarily cautious, and overly solicitous of the Administration.[3] This criticism was evidently true. But what were the reasons for this fact? What were the forces that caused these formal institutions to deviate so far from their normal institutional function? Facts tell us that it was the accumulated and mobilized social power in the form of informal interpersonal power dynamics that shaped the institutional operation. Nixon and his men's power of interpersonal connections were so strong that the system with all its institutional means would not work unless the opposite side effectively mobilized its power in a similar form; i.e., the system only worked after the Nixon interpersonal power encountered effective resistance and counter-offensive from the Washington collective power in the form of informal interpersonal networks. The FBI and the CIA investigation into the Watergate affair at this stage reflected the strong networking force inside and outside the formal institutions.

In their investigation of the break-in, FBI agents logically focused on McCord's links, trying to determine who had hired him, what money was available to him, and who worked with him. From the very beginning, FBI efforts to move beyond the basic seven suspects were shadowed and even shaped by Nixon's interpersonal connections and eventually surrendered to the interpersonal power dynamics.

First, the Nixon power was mobilized in the form of interpersonal connections and based on interpersonal power dynamics in its own ranks. People in the Nixon camp worked hard to safeguard the Nixon power regardless of whether their behavior was legal or illegal. They paid even less attention to their institutional roles as government officials. The reason was that the Nixon power was still powerful enough to offer incentives for people to strive to be socially associated with it. The expectation that Nixon would be elected to another term enhanced his power. People's actions were following the strength of power until the power was no longer powerful enough as a social mechanism to offer what they desired. The state institutions, or the "system", were only a site of the power struggle. They had no independent power to dominate actors' actions. As Kutler recorded, the FBI agents' interviews with White House officials, such as Charles Colson, were repeatedly disturbed by White House Counsel John Dean in a quarrelsome manner. When agents spoke to campaign officials, CREEP lawyers stayed in the room and constantly interfered with the process. The agents conducted more than sixty interviews at CREEP headquarters, but could not get the truth. Important witnesses like Mitchell and Magruder committed perjury. Liddy's secretary, Robert Odle, the CREEP director of administration, waited ten months before revealing that he had hidden the Gemstone file from investigators. Evidence had been destroyed, and specifically, Liddy had shredded documents. Agents got circumstantial information but they simply could not prove the destruction. Nearly a year later, Mitchell described for the Senate Select Committee the White House determination in "keeping the lid on and no information volunteered." Those interviewed had been coached to lie. They even rehearsed testimonies.[4]

Second, the Nixon power was reflected in its informal form by its interpersonal power dynamics to those institutions that were duty-bound to investigate the Nixon camp. This was the source of the inept behavior of those government institutions. The FBI knew that it had been wrong to allow Dean to sit in during interviews and to clear all requests for information. But, did they have an alternative? No, because they were in a power structure that was, at that period, dominated by the Nixon force. The investigatory procedure had been determined by FBI Acting Director Gray, who had a trusting personal relationship with Nixon. Therefore, the FBI investigation proceeded under heavy White House influence. Furthermore, Gray routinely submitted FBI investigative reports to Dean, which enabled the White House aide to keep abreast of the investigation. The collaborative relationship between Gray and Dean was good to the extent that Dean gave Gray important evidence belonging to Howard Hunt and Gray withheld and later destroyed this evidence.[5]

The CIA also played softly and tenderly to the Nixon camp. Deputy Director of the CIA Vernon Walters was Nixon's man at the CIA. His relationship with Nixon could be dated back fifteen years. Walters had performed secret missions for Nixon on many occasions and had been his personal translator in foreign diplomatic negotiations off and on. CIA Director Helms even suspected that Walters was sent over to the CIA early in 1972 specifically for the purpose of gathering intelligence for Nixon about him. Walters knew how to keep his month shut and was, therefore, the best man for the job. Haldeman met Walters on June 23rd, and hours later, Walters and FBI's Gray sat down and made an arrangement.

Walters did not provide anything definite. Gray did not ask anything definite. Walters did not tell Gray that Watergate was a CIA operation. He did not explicitly ask the FBI to stop its investigation. He knew the way political actors played the survivors' game. It was clear, at least to Walters and Helms, that Nixon's power was not omnipresent and not powerful enough to cover them against Nixon's enemy's attack. Walters only told Gray that the FBI's efforts to trace the burglar's money through a Mexican bank account might hurt the CIA's operations in Mexico. Pat Gray also knew the survival game. He did not expect direct statements. The CIA did not have to make the demand explicit. "Maybes" would be good enough to put FBI investigators on hold and constrain them from going any further. The FBI got an excuse: they did not want to ruin a CIA operation south of the border.

Once Walters provided Gray with the excuse he needed, matters were arranged. The FBI's investigation of the Watergate burglar's money trial suddenly stopped one crucial step short of connecting the Watergate burglars' money with Liddy and the Committee to Re-Elect the President. This was a delicately constructed balance based upon a realistic analysis of the power parity at that point in time. But then Nixon's people, Haldeman, Ehrlichman, and Dean, arrogant as they always were, decided to press their advantage even further. Walters and Helms had given them something, but they wanted more. They were driven by the arrogance of power and trapped themselves in an unrealistic miscalculation.

John Ehrlichman told Dean to demand more. On June 26th, 27th, and 28th, Dean told Walters, and through him, Helms, that he was not satisfied about the CIA's careful going along. The CIA would have to take over entire operational responsibility and to payoff the burglars and the whole program.

This was a mistake. Were they capable of mobilizing enough power to back up their demands and support Walters or Helms if anything went wrong? They miscalculated the strength of their own power and overlooked the strength of the potential collective power in Washington. But Helms and Walters knew better. In a power game, a demand must correspond with the strength of power. If a demand was too far beyond the "reasonable zone" where the power could reach, the demand itself would only be a sign of weakness. Helms and Walters knew that to make such an unreasonable demand only meant that Nixon was in deep trouble. They sensed that Nixon was not in complete control of those powerful politicians and he was vulnerable in a serious investigation. Therefore he was in danger of losing power along the way. Based upon the evaluation of the strength of power, they didn't mortgage any more of their fate in order to avoid making themselves fair game for Nixon's powerful opponents. The CIA retreated from further involvement.

The strategy Walters and Helms used to accomplish their retreat was simple: they demanded that Nixon first show his strength of power before asking anything further of them. Vernon Walters told John Dean that the CIA would not cover-up for Nixon without an explicit presidential order to do so. It was clear that if Nixon were bold enough to issue such an order, it would be a sign of strength; it would be possible that he would be able to protect the CIA as an agency and Helms and Walters as individuals. However, if no presidential order was forthcoming, it would be a sign of weakness. Nixon's opponents would be powerful enough to scare Nixon off from involving himself directly in the cover-up.[6]

The FBI had another type of power game. By July 5th, Gray burned Hunt's dirty-tricks files for John Dean; this action demonstrated the depth of his personal loyalty to Nixon. But he faced an in-house insurrection by FBI agents who were angry at delays in the Watergate investigation. Although he was formally the director of the agency, the exact same institutional position as his predecessor, J. Edgar Hoover, as a newcomer to the well-constructed J. Edgar Hoover's turf, Gray did not have deeply rooted informal power in the bureau to keep his agents on leash. He had far less informal power both inside the FBI and in the political world in general. What his formal institutional position allowed him to do was only keep a passive attitude toward the investigation while helping the White House under the table. He did not have the informal power beyond his institutional position to stop the investigation. Here, it was clear that institutional position did not automatically bestow power to its occupants and transform power into authority. Power depended on how much resource could be mobilized in both formal and informal ways. The comparison between Hoover and Gray clearly showed how powerful and significant the informal way was.

After all, either the FBI's or the CIA's leaders could have opposed Nixon actively. Although they did not help Nixon as much as he wanted them to, they did not do anything to expose Nixon's illegal activities either, as their institutional functions required them to. The reason was that the White House did not convince them that the Nixon camp had enough power to cover them if anything went wrong. But, at the same time, the power of the White House was still there, powerful enough to make the FBI's Gray continue to funnel up-to-the-minute information about the progress of his agents' investigations to Dean at the White House, and he continued to tell Dean about leads that were being uncovered—all of which allowed the White House to alter its cover-up plans accordingly.

The CIA, meanwhile, sat passively on the sidelines. For example, it did not inform anybody that former agent Howard Hunt had made use of CIA hardware when he was involved in the other break-in at Daniel Ellsberg's psychiatrist's office in the name of plugging leaks for the reason of "national security," ten months before Watergate. At this stage of the power struggle, the CIA and FBI made no move to broaden Watergate case beyond Hunt's and Liddy's level, even though the legal evidence was there already. Even though the amateur investigators, the two *Washington Post* reporters, uncovered Liddy's secret CREEP fund, which had financed the burglars, as early as in July and August. Those professional FBI men who tried to reach Hunt and Liddy were sabotaged by the director of their agency. The CIA directors, meanwhile, kept silent about all the under table dealings they had with Haldeman, Dean and Ehrlichman. They did nothing to disturb the cover-up.[7]

THE INSTITUTIONAL FUNCTION OF THE JUSTICE DEPARTMENT

At the time when the FBI and the CIA were circling around without much real progress, overall responsibility for the investigation belonged to the Department of Justice. The criminal division charged the whole operation. Assistant Attorney General Henry Petersen, a career government official, headed the division. He maintained contact with Acting FBI director Gray and with the U.S. Attorney's office in Washington. Under the direction of U.S. Attorney Harold Titus, assistant U.S. Attorney Earl Silbert was in charge of the day-to-day prosecutorial investigation. Later, after Hunt and Liddy had been implicated, Seymour Glanzer and Donald Compbell joined him.

As career bureaucrats in the Justice Department, those federal prosecutors working on the Watergate case for recently appointed Attorney General Kleindienst were confined in the break-in case. CREEP had been a focus of investigation after CREEP's Liddy joined CREEP's security director James McCord in the Watergate net. However, CREEP was John Mitchell's turf. John Mitchell was former Attorney General and current Attorney Kleindienst owed his job to Mitchell.

Several hours after the burglary, Liddy turned up at a Washington golf course to see Attorney General Kleindienst. According to Kleindienst, Liddy said that Mitchell wanted the Attorney General to get the suspects out of jail at once. Kleindienst claimed he did not believe Mitchell would send such a message and publicly threatened to have Liddy arrested. But he told no one of the incident. The FBI later claimed that if he did so, it would have more easily identified Liddy as an important actor in the events and they would have had reason to zero in early on Mitchell and Liddy. And therefore, the cover-up might have been more quickly exposed.[8]

A conversation between Kleindienst and Dean revealed depth of the personal relationship between Kleindienst and Mitchell. Dean recorded: "I [Dean] watched him [Kleindienst] change moods as he stared silently at his desk.'If John Mitchell is in trouble,' he said gravely, 'I'll resign before I'd ever prosecute him.'"[9]

The same conversation and the conversation between Dean and Petersen exposed the typical attitude of the political leaders and the high-rank career bureaucrats in the Justice Department toward the investigation. When Dean told both Kleindienst and Petersen about the fact that "I don't believe the White House can stand a wide-open investigation," "if this investigation leads into the White House, I'm afraid the President may not be reelected. There's so much shit going on there, "he got assurance that Earl Silbert got the case and had been instructed that he was investigating a break-in and not supposed to "wander off beyond his authority into other things." Having known that the case had been limited to the break-in only, Dean felt a great relief.[10]

The first stage power contest in formal government agencies based on rather informal power dynamics produced the first stage result of the investigation. On September 15, the indictments were handed down by the grand jury. As expected, Hunt, Liddy and the five men arrested on June 17 were indicted. The seven were charged with as many as eight separate counts each but all centered on the case of break-in. The preorchestrated fanfare was heavy. Kleindienst said the investigation was "one of the most intensive, objective, and thorough investigations in many years, reaching out to cities all across the United States as well as into foreign countries."[11] The Justice Department's conclusion was: "We have absolutely no evidence to indicate that any others should be charged." The new Re-election Committee Chairman after John Mitchell, Clark MacGregor, called on "those who have recklessly sought to connect others with the case" to "publicly apologize for their unfounded charges." Senator Robert Dole, the Republican Party chairman, said the indictments proved "there is no evidence to substantiate any of the wild and slanderous statements McGovern has been making about many high officials in the Nixon Administration." Congressman Gerald R. Ford, the House Republican leader, said the indictments reinforced his "understanding that none of the people in the White House, in positions of leadership in the party or [in] the Committee to Re-elect the President were involved."[12]

However, some *Washington Post* journalists noted that the indictments did "not touch on the central questions about the purpose or sponsorship of the alleged espionage." "Berstein, Woodward and the editors had become increasingly skeptical of the federal investigation. Why weren't the $89,000 in Mexican checks, the $25,000 Dahlberg check and the Stans slush fund mentioned in the indictment? How could the indictment be so limited if the government had the same information as the Post?"[13]

The perception that the Justice Department's investigation was compromised was not without reason, but that was before the transformation of the case from break-in to cover-up soon after the creation of the Senate Committee. As professional bureaucrats, they worked only in the scope determined by the informal power dynamics. As Silbert, the Assistant U.S Attorney who was in charge of the Watergate case from its beginning to Cox taking over, later confirmed to this point: first, during the several months following the break-in, Watergate was a matter that only received some attention from the D.C. press. The powerful political leaders had not connected; therefore the scope which determined the investigation was set simply in the scope of break-in. Secondly, because Watergate was a break-in, at least that was what the prosecutors perceived it to be, they did their job in terms of breaking the break-in case. "For the break-in, the burglary, and the wiretap, the liability, at least as established in a court of law, has only been established at a level one rung above Mr. Liddy. That was, of course, Mr. Magruder." (Silbert, in Friedman, 1992: 49) So, as long as the case was not about the cover-up and the obstruction of justice, Watergate would continue to mean break-in. Therefore, a professional bureaucrat like Silbert had no way to target the people who occupied the high positions. "It is for the cover-up and obstruction of justice that the people with the highest positions in government or former high positions were subsequently indicted and properly convicted."[14] According to Silbert, the combination of serious offenses in the Watergate scandal which were later defined as the true nature of the case were only exposed after the scope of the investigation was redefined.[15]

Dean, as the person who was in the position to coordinate the cover-up, was pleased. "Phase one of the cover-up was a success. The doors that led to Magruder, Mitchell and many others were closed, at least for the present."[16]

Surely Nixon, at that time, was still in a dominate position in the power dynamics. He still had strong power of rewarding and sanctioning. He had much to offer to his personal, instead of institutional, loyalists and possessed the power to punish those who were bold enough to challenge him whereas Democratic presidential nominee, Senator George McGovern, was much less powerful in this type of interpersonal power dynamics. Dean thus got dizzy with success: "I was sitting in an Administration in which a dozen high officials were guilty of criminal violations that I knew of, and I watched the President's lead in the polls climb steadily: roughly twenty points ahead in August and still rising."[17]

For the moment, then, the bureaucratic elite whose institutional functions were to investigate and punish those wrong-doers held back. Because leaks were carefully handled, few, even within Washington, yet grasped Watergate as a whole. Their chances of doing so now depended upon the overall power dynamics between the Nixon camp and its opponents in the form of the interpersonal power of connections. Whoever mobilized stronger interpersonal power would gain upper hand in the Washington collective power dynamics and therefore get help from the federal agencies, as well as the entire criminal justice system. Socially embedded power dynamics were effective here. In a highly risky and uncertain political environment, interpersonal networks would become more reliable and more rewarding for power players.

THE PATMAN INVESTIGATION

The next day, after the arrest of five Watergate burglars, Democratic Party chairman O'Brien filed a $1 million civil damage suit against the Committee for the Re-election of the President. O'Brien charged that the facts were "developing a clear line to the White House."[18] This would be the very first push to change the power dynamics among those powerful politicians that finally drove Nixon from office.

Four days after the break-in, Senator William Proxmire (D-WI) joined the inquiry about Watergate. He asked Federal Reserve Board Chairman Arthur Burns for the name of the banks involved in issuing the cash found on the burglars. Burns refused. The next day, Congressman Patman for the first time involved himself in this matter. He seconded Proxmire's request, but Burns again declined.[19]

Patman, a Texas fellow with a reputation as a loner, had his institutional power base in the House Banking and Currency Committee, in which he was the Chairman. In the meantime, his strong influence in the House's power structure was rooted in the fact that he was one of the shrewdest congressional barons for a long time. As early as in the 1940s when Lyndon Johnson went to Washington, his father told him to watch and follow Patman. Patman, as a strong man, had the interpersonal connections and influence to embed his institutional function. He thus had the resources to make waves and surf on them. But, at the same time, his informal power was limited because, as it was widely known, Patman was a loner. The formal function of his committee was greatly influenced by this fact and the fate of his formal investigation was thus determined.

Patman's planned hearings on the Watergate money transactions posed the biggest threat to Nixon at the time when Nixon's popularity was high and the re-election campaign, together with the cover-up of Watergate break-in, was very successful. Patman focused his attention on Maurice Stans, the CREEP finance chairman. Patman and his staff believed that as the chief financier of the Committee to Re-elect the President, Stans was a key link between CREEP and the break-in.[20]

Nixon recognized how serious the hearings could be. His strategy was to stretch his informal interpersonal power. He instructed Dean to ask Jerry Ford, the minority leader in the House, to block the hearings. According to Dean, Nixon said: "This is the big play." "I'm getting into this thing, so that he [Ford], he's got to know that it comes from the top—and that he's got to get at this and screw this thing up while he can, right?"[21]

A conversation between Haldeman and Dean about the Patman hearings revealed the social dynamics in the political process. Dean:

"I've been talking to Bill Timmons and Stans and Petersen on this thing, and Mitchell is working on it, too. . . . We really need to turn Patman off."

"Call Connally," said Haldeman. "He may know some way to stop Patman. And tell Timmons to keep on Jerry Ford's ass. He knows he's got to produce on this one."[22]

Dean then talked to Connally about the Patman hearings. Connally immediate understood his intension and provided a lead for him. He understood "from the grapevine down in Texas that Patman might have a couple of weak spots," "I believe I heard the Congressman received some contributions from an oil lobbyist up here. I don't believe Mr. Patman has reported them." Dean seemed to have found the switch to turn Patman off.[23]

Dean started to work on this matter. According to his description, over the next several weeks, he and many others in the administration worked hard through informal interpersonal connections to move the formal institutions toward a direction that would be able to block the Patman investigation. Ken Parkinson, attorney for the CREEP and for Stans, was assigned to check into the reported contributions to Patman and the other members of this committee. Mitchell was working with "some Rockefeller people" to bring pressure on the New York members of the committee.[24]

On September 26, Dean got a memorandum from Kenneth Parkinson. This memorandum detailed the House committee members' campaign-finance reports and the political action committee that contributed to members' campaigns. This behind-the-scene hard work provided a weapon for Dean: the Banking and Currency Committee's members themselves had not wholly complied with the law. He promised Nixon that if anyone wanted "to play rough," the White House would not hesitate to respond in kind. Dean proposed nothing less than blackmail.[25]

Driven by informal interpersonal power dynamics, the formal institutions started working toward undoing the institutional duty. Under the pressure from the White House, Henry Petersen finally gave in and started to play the good guy. He wrote an official Justice Department letter objecting to the hearings on the grounds that the publicity of the hearing would endanger the rights of Liddy and other Watergate defendants at the trial. Based upon this high-sounding reasoning, all the Republican members of the committee began to make civil-liberty speeches. They claimed that they wouldn't vote to investigate Watergate because they wanted Liddy to get a fair trial.

The counterassault to Patman's investigation began on September 4. Republicans in the committee refused to cooperate in the forthcoming investigation. On September 11, Stans declined the invitation to appear before the committee.

Patman was furious. He told Stans's attorney that his client's refusal to appear amounted to "a high level decision . . . to continue a massive cover-up and to do everything possible to hinder a full-scale public airing of the Watergate case." He made his determination clear that this "first political espionage case" in American history "must not be swept under the rug."[26] This was the first time the charge of cover-up was formally brought up. To get the bottom of this suspicious fact, Patman told his colleagues that the committee needed subpoena power. Patman's committee could do nothing if it lacked subpoena powers. But Patman did not have the support of his full committee.

At the Oct. 3rd Banking and Currency Committee meeting, Patman pointed out that charges and allegations about "the greatest political espionage case" in American history reached "right into the White House" but the White House had obstructed his staff's efforts. He thus made it very clear that the target of his investigation was the White House and the struggle was between him and the White House over the issue of cover-up.

The Republicans in the Banking and Currency Committee were unified to oppose any investigation. To make the situation worse for Patman, the significant power imbalance came from within Patman's own ranks—from conservative Southern Democrats and from two northerners who normally would not be opponents.[27]

In a field where power was vital and money, in turn, was a key source of power, few people could claim to be clean. There was a strong force to push people in the system to collect more and more money in order to gain more and more power. In a field like this, prying into campaign irregularities was, to be sure, a potentially embarrassing subject for a variety of powerful politicians, especially during a campaign. Patman's very goal created Patman Committee's impasses. Two Northerners, Brasco and Hanna, defected and their defection surprised Patman. The defection highlighted how informal interpersonal power defeated Patman's formal institutional power.

Brasco had been the target of an investigation of alleged fraud and bribery activities since 1970. Armed with this knowledge, John Mitchell used his personal connections in New York to pressure Brasco's defection. He arranged a meeting with Brasco and a New York City Democratic leader. The topic was Brasco's role in the House Banking and Currency Committee proceedings. Mitchell mobilized his interpersonal resources to an extent that New York Governor Nelson Rockefeller was involved. He later admitted that he had helped Mitchell arrange a meeting at that time between Mitchell, Brasco, and a Democratic leader. Mitchell's efforts resulted in "assurances" that Brasco would not appear at the crucial committee meetings or would oppose Patman.

As early as November 24th, 1971, J. Edgar Hoover told Mitchell that Korean lobbyist Park Tongsun had made campaign payments to Congressman Hanna and that the money had originated with the Korean CIA. In another memo dating from early 1972, Hoover reported that Hanna had actively solicited payments from Park. Accepting foreign money for a Congressman would be a serious crime against the system. But the powerful politicians did nothing to punish the criminal behavior at the time. Rather, they just used it as their resource in a power dynamics. Hanna thus became Nixon's man in the battle between Nixon and Patman.

For the Southern Democrats, the opposition to Patman was more personal. The leader of the committee's southerners, Stephens, had close ties with the Administration. In the next six months after the destruction of the Patman investigation, he received an extraordinary amount of patronage from Nixon. Another Banking and Currency Committee member, William Chappell, was in a tight race for election that year. He cleverly used his formal institutional position as a resource to exchange for the more powerful and effective informal interpersonal power from the President. Before the committee's vote, he visited privately with the President and then had a photo session. Because McGovern was immensely unpopular in Chappell's district, the photo session would be an important help. Also, one of the Congressman's secretaries alleged in 1969 that Chappell had forced her to kick back some of her salary and Chappell acknowledged a "technical error." His close tie with the Administration protected him from this criminal behavior; the Justice Department decided not to prosecute.

The Republican Leaders in Congress helped at this point. House Minority Leader Gerald Ford played some informal and negative role in the Patman investigation. A few days before the House committee vote, Ford wrote to Republican members urging them to attend the committee meeting "to assure that the investigative resolution is appropriately drawn." Congresswoman Margaret Heckler, a member of the committee, stated that Ford had relayed White House assurance that Hunt and Liddy alone had perpetrated the Watergate "caper." He also met with other members of the Banking and Currency Committee. In addition, Ford charged that Patman had started a "political witch hunt" and offered his own assurances that no one in the White House or CREEP had been involved.[28]

Back-room power dynamics finally destroyed the Patman investigation. On October 3, the Banking and Currency Committee voted 20-15 to deny Chairman Patman subpoena power for his Watergate investigation. That ended any chance of a congressional inquiry before the election. Although Patman proceeded without subpoenas, as Kutler vividly describes: it was a futile gesture. His public hearing on October 10 "ended up with lecturing four empty chairs with big name plates in front of them marked 'Mr. Mitchell,' 'Mr. MacGregor,' 'Mr. Stans' and 'Mr. Dean.' A bitter Patman warned: 'The fight is not over.'"[29]

Patman's earlier attempts to reframe the Watergate case from break-in to cover-up failed. On the macro-level, the reason was the distractions of the political campaign. His investigation was framed as partisan. But the micro-level interpersonal power dynamics really produced the outcome. It was clear that Nixon overpowered Patman by having interpersonally unified the Republican members of the House Banking Committee and further enlisted

Southern and Northern Democrats. The reason for Nixon to achieve this would be that Nixon's social power in and through interpersonal networks had not met its match. His behavior hurt most people in the high circle but they had not developed effective collective power to counter his interpersonal power. Only when Nixon's adversaries had effectively mobilized, the collective power dynamics would eventually overwhelm Nixon's interpersonal power. Before this collective power dynamics took shape, Putman's institutional power seemed hollow and powerless. The Nixon camp still seemed very powerful to attract those who were eager to be enlisted interpersonally in order to benefit from the advancement and the protection Nixon could offer; at the same time, the Nixon camp was still powerful enough to exert pressure on those who were excluded from such a powerful establishment. In routine politics, the exclusion from a powerful interpersonal networks centered on powerful politicians was seen as a punishment. The troops were not effectively mobilized on the Patman side. Nixon's power to offer and power to punish via interpersonal connections were still appearing strong.

Patman's inquiry accomplished nothing in the immediate sense, but its attempt to reframing the Watergate case as cover-up directly confronted CREEP and the White House. It thus had some important consequences. By reframing the Watergate case as a cover-up, in addition to a break-in, his investigation pioneered a collective power dynamic among powerful politicians. This reframing aimed at mobilizing collective power among power politicians drove the Nixon camp to a new level of exhausting its interpersonal capital and networking resources for mobilizing congressional support. The provocation in its somewhat coercive interpersonal relationships with congressmen showed a sign of the fatigue of the Nixon camp. Patman was wounded institutionally but still live and well in the collectivity of powerful politicians. What Nixon and his men could do was only frustrating Patman's institutional investigation and overwhelming his interpersonal networking resources. But their interpersonal power could not fundamentally damage the power base Patman had built up over the years in Congress and in the collectivity of the powerful politicians. He still had the resources to stage a comeback once the collective power dynamics were mobilized. Several months later, he ordered his staff to share its materials and findings with Senator Sam Ervin and the newly created Senate Select Committee. Patman himself wrote to Ervin on the issue of questioning Dean for his interference with the House Banking and Currency Committee investigation. Speaker of the House Carl Albert believed that Nixon lived "in constant torture" from the moment Wright Patman's Banking and Currency Committee began its investigation. Patman started something, Albert said, that made Nixon's life a living hell from then on. He knew that this thing had been done, he knew that . . . there had been a cover-up and he had not stopped it. He was afraid all the time that they might find that out. So he must have had a life of real misery.[30]

This "something" that Patman started was the collective power dynamics in the high circle of powerful politicians.

THE MEDIA AND PUBLIC REACTIONS

The American political system bestows upon the press an important role to be instructive but only if the powerful political leaders frame the issue coherently and persistently. The mass media in any political controversy have the institutional function to create a bystander public, to involve the onlookers in the dispute. The media also provides the political actors on both sides with a looking glass image of how they appear to the public. However, a strange phenomenon was that media interest in the Watergate affair was much less than it should have been. Of the three television networks, only NBC assigned one of its Washington reporters full time to the story. There were more than 430 reporters in Washington news bureaus for different newspapers and media outlets, only fewer than 15 of them worked exclusively on Watergate. Until March and April 1973, very few newspapers gave Watergate any sustained attention. *The New York Times* did not continuously report on the Watergate case until January 1973. The *Washington Post* was unique in its continuing coverage of unfolding events. The *Chicago Tribune* did not feature a Watergate story on its front page until August 27.[31]

The stifling of Patman's investigation in October 1972 effectively took Watergate off the front pages. George McGovern tried to exploit the issue in the institutional framework of two party system. But he could not attract serious attention. His comparisons to Teapot Dome sounded hysterical, even absurd, in the eyes of the media people. Instead of focusing on Watergate and Nixon's other problems, the press paid more attention to the psychiatric treatment of Senator George McGovern's running mate, Senator Eagleton. It was no wonder that of the nation's 753 daily papers, more than 70 percent endorsed Richard Nixon that November, versus 56, only 5 percent, that endorsed McGovern.[32]

However, as the Longs pointed out, there is no reason to conclude that the media coverage was not sufficient to have made clear majorities of the public aware of the Watergate affair during the presidential campaign. When Gallup asked in September 1972, "Have you read or heard about Watergate?"

52 percent of a national sample said they had.[33] And by October, 87 percent of the voters in Summit County, Ohio, said they were aware of the "Watergate break-in."[34]

It was clear that awareness was far from enough for most citizens to take any action in a political struggle like Watergate. For a complex case that could not be easily understood, this lack of comprehensive and sustained reporting crippled most people outside of a small circle of powerful people in Washington to think about the true meaning of this case. Network television news, as a visual medium, could only communicate a sense, a mood; it could not clarify the complicated legal and constitutional aspects of Watergate. It was not until TV cameras were let into the hearings of the Senate Watergate Committee, which was designed to frame the case legally and politically in front of the citizenry in general, that the nature of Watergate affair as it was defined and framed by those powerful politicians made sense to most of the citizens in the public domain. Although the basic facts that later became such a familiar part of the Watergate saga had been publicized and most citizens were aware of them, media attention at that time had played little role in transforming Watergate from the circle of those powerful politicians to citizens in general. Watergate was not on the public agenda for a long time.

The action of the mass media just reflected the current collective power dynamics. At that time before the turn of the New Year, the Nixon camp was still in control in the power dynamics; its opponents were still in a state of disarray. Bureaucratic agencies, and the whole criminal justice system, were under the power of Nixon while felt little pressure from Nixon's opponents. In a word, the power struggle centering on Watergate among the powerful politicians had just gotten started; the organized citizens in bureaucratic and media arenas were still struggling in making sense of it from the fragmentary and less coherent signals offered by those powerful politicians. For those unorganized citizens, they could only see the Watergate scandal as "politics as usual," just pots calling kettles black. It was impossible for them to think about other interpretations at that time.

In a situation where ordinary citizens had no direct and immediate interest to fight for, nor did the culture they lived in have a clear precedent to guide them to react, the key would be how the Watergate affair would be literally framed and socially constructed. Watergate was one of those issues requiring sustained and coherent media coverage for citizens both organized and unorganized to get what those political leaders wanted them to know and to understand what they wanted them to do. Citizens would be outraged and prepared to charge the Nixon administration the political price for its various trespasses only when the political leaders had led them to know the "whole facts" and after the political leaders framed the facts in a fashion that they could symbolically make sense of. Citizens, even those organized ones, needed to be led to know the whole nature of the story; otherwise, like most of the political stories, it would be regarded as outside the range of and remote from their immediate concerns. In addition, unlike most organized citizens who were very sensitive to their lion's share of the system, unorganized citizens had little motivation to even think about the damage done to the system by the Nixon Administration. Because it was highly unlikely for anyone to expect anything else based on the information and the frame of the information most people could get at that time, who cared about Watergate outside Washington? Public-opinion polls consistently confirmed the general impression that Watergate was not serious at all. It was only a "Washington story."[35]

NIXON AT THE ZENITH OF HIS INSTITUTIONAL POWER

The results of the November 7, 1972 presidential election were not surprising. Nixon had an enormous advantage based on his interpersonal power over Senator McGovern. Nixon won by a landslide. He beat McGovern by almost two-to-one. He won 61 percent of the ballots and swept every electoral vote except those of Massachusetts and the District of Columbia. And more significantly, Nixon also shattered familiar voting behavior patterns: 55 percent of blue-collar workers voted for him, 51 percent of union families, and 37 percent of registered Democrats. Traditionally Democratic ethnics—Italians, Poles, Irish, and Jews—voted for Nixon in unprecedented numbers.[36]

Nixon was at the zenith of his institutional power. The interpersonal power dynamics in Washington had made the state formal institutions serve his ends so far. But he failed to pay enough attention to a fundamental fact that institutional power must be embedded in the Washington collective power dynamics. The strength of institutional power to a large extent depends on how deeply it is rooted in collectively coded social connections. Nixon was about to pay dearly because of this mistake.

NOTES

1. Hargrove, Erwin C. *The Missing Link.* (Washington, D.C.: Urban Institute, 1975), 114.

2. Cole, Richard and David Caputo, "Presidential Control of the Senior Civil Service," *American Political Review* 73 (June 1979), 399–412.

3. Ervin, Sam Jr. *The Whole Truth: The Watergate Conspiracy.* (New York: Random House, 1980), 12.

4. Kutler, Stanley I. *The Wars of Watergate: The Last Crisis of Richard Nixon.* (New York: Knopf, 1990), 209–210.

5. Kutler, *The Wars of Watergate,* 209–211.

6. All the CIA story cited here can be found in Congressional Quarterly Inc. *Watergate: Chronology of a Crisis.*(Washington D.C.: Congressional Quarterly Press, 1975), appendix: 89A-91A; Powers, Thomas. *The Man Who Kept the Secrets: Richard Helms and the CIA.* (New York: Knopf, Pocket Books reprint, 1981), 325–478.

7. McQuaid, Kim. *The Anxious Years—America in the Vietnam-Watergate era.* (New York: Basic Books, 1989), 188–191.

8. Kleindienst, Richard. *Justice: The Memoirs of an Attorney General.* (Ottawa, IL: Jameson Books, 1985), 46.

9. Dean, John W. III. *Blind Ambition: The White House Years.* (New York: Simon & Shuster, 1976), 109.

10. Dean, *Blind Ambition,* 110–113

11. Bernstein, Carl and Bob Woodward. *All the President's Men.* (New York: Simon & Shuster, 1974), 69.

12. Dean, *Blind Ambition,* 133.

13. Bernstein and Woodward, *All the President's Men,* 69.

14. Silbert, Earl J. Panel Discussion on Watergate and the Abuse of Presidential Power. in Friedman, Leon and William F. Levantrosser (eds.) *Watergate and Afterward —the legacy of Richar M. Nixon.* (Westport, Connecticut & London: Greenwood Press, 1992), 49.

15. Silbert, Earl J. in Friedman and Levantrosser, 49–50.

16. Dean, *Blind Ambition,* 133.

17. Dean, *Blind Ambition,* 128.

18. Bernstein and Woodward, *All the President's Men,* 26.

19. Kutler, *The Wars of Watergate,* 227.

20. Kutler, *The Wars of Watergate,* 227–229.

21. Dean, *Blind Ambition,* 139.

22. Dean, *Blind Ambition,* 142.

23. Dean, *Blind Ambition,* 142.

24. Dean, *Blind Ambition,* 142–144.

25. Kutler, *The Wars of Watergate,* 230–231.

26. Kutler, *The Wars of Watergate,* 230.

27. Kutler, *The Wars of Watergate,* 229–231.

28. Kutler, *The Wars of Watergate,* 231–233; Dean, *Blind Ambition,* 144.

29. Kutler, *The Wars of Watergate,* 234.

30. Kutler, *The Wars of Watergate,* 227.

31. Kutler, *The Wars of Watergate,* 226.

32. Kutler, *The Wars of Watergate,* 226; McQuaid, Kim. *The Anxious Years—America in the Vietnam-Watergate era.* (New York: Basic Books, 1989), 194; Schell, Jonathan. *The Time of Illusion: An Historical and Reflective Account of the Vietnam Era.* (New York: Vintage Books, 1976), 287.

33. Lang, Gladys Engel and Kurt Lang. *The Battle for Public Opinion—the President, the press, and the polls during Watergate.* (New York: Columbia University Press, 1983), 32–33

34. Mendelsohn, Harold and Garrett J. O'Keefe. *The People Choose a President.* (New York: Praeger, 1976), 200.

35. Kutler, *The Wars of Watergate*, 236.

36. Kutler, The Wars of Watergate, 237.

Chapter Two

The Formation of the Collective Power Dynamics

THE CREATION OF THE ERVIN COMMITTEE

It was widely spread in Washington after the New Year about the involvement of the President's men in the White House or the Committee for Reelection of the President in the Watergate break-in. But by the end of 1972 the highest campaign official indicted by the grand jury was G. Gordon Liddy. No evidence was found that might touch the President or his White House staff or any high-ups in the CREEP. I agree with the insightful assertion by historian Kutler that "Watergate might have remained as the story-that-never-was had it not been for the determination of Mike Mansfield and Sam Ervin."[1]

The driving force behind the effort to get to the bottom of Watergate was neither from the media nor public opinion nor the criminal justice system. The driving force was the social dynamics that reflected the collective power of powerful politicians in the US Senate. This collective power dynamic fundamentally changed the course of the Watergate investigation and effectively redressed the issue of illegality.

The conflict pitted the White House against those powerful politicians who wanted full disclosure of the facts behind the illegal attempt to plant wiretaps in the national headquarters of the Democratic Party. At first, these powerful politicians included the Democrat's Chairman who sought publicity as well as redress through a civil suit. After the New Year of 1973, many powerful senators in the United States Senate got involved.

Senate Majority Leader Mike Mansfield made a pledge to his constituents back in Montana during the 1972 campaign that he would "pave the way" for an investigation of the Watergate break-in in particular and the illegal campaign practice in general. Mansfield had been working hard, after the election, behind the scenes to mobilize the Washington collective power to launch an investigation in the Senate on those suspicions and speculations about Watergate and the possible involvement of the White House. What factor motivated him and made him use his immense power to mobilize the authority as the majority leader in a powerful institution? Mansfield had no personal bitterness for Nixon. But he was embittered by the attacks on his old friends Senators Hubert Humphrey and Edmund Muskie. He disliked "those dirty letters people wrote about them" and was disturbed by the Watergate break-in, "which went beyond the guidelines of American politics."[2] It was clear that Nixon hurt many of Mansfield's friends by violating the collectively accepted codes of political conduct. Mansfield was offended.

As Ervin described Mansfield's intention: "After the election, he expressed to me his concern about some of the publicly known 'dirty tricks' which had been practiced on Senators Humphrey, Jackson, Muskie, and McGovern during the primary and election campaigns."[3]

It would be clear that Nixon offended many powerful Senators during the campaign. Each of these senators had his own strong power base. Their political move would gain strong support from multi-layered vast networks. However, it was their collective power that was very formidable. Senator Edward Kennedy had begun a preliminary investigation of the Watergate matter through his Administrative Practices Subcommittee in October 1972. But since he was not a person who could generate and sustain this collective power, his investigation went nowhere. As Senator Kennedy told Woodward, he knew little, if anything, more than that what he had read in the papers. "But I know the people around Nixon," he said, "and that's enough. They're thugs."[4] The collective power dynamics required someone who was the right person, at the right place, and at the right time to stimulate the collective process.

It was not easy to do this in Washington. "To investigate Watergate meant that Mansfield would have to move the investigation through the snares of internal congressional politics."[5] Institutionally speaking, it was the duty of the Judiciary Committee of the Senate to conduct such an investigation. However, the Chairman of the Senate Judiciary Committee was Senator James O. Eastland of Mississippi, who had a reputation as a loyalist to Nixon. He used to boast that "I get any damn thing I wanted" from Nixon ranging from appointments to other privilege or patronage.[6] The system would not work under such a circumstance. Formalistic institutional checks and balances surrendered to the substantive power of personal connections; separation of powers was overwhelmed by the omnipresence of interpersonal power-sharing. Mansfield needed to develop an informal network to fulfill the formal duty. Informal networks here played a much more decisive role than the institutional construction to set the collective power dynamics on the course.

The only thing Mansfield could do if he wanted to proceed would be lifting the investigation out of the formal institutional construction, i.e., out of the routine Senate procedures and organizational channels. Only in this way could he get around Eastland's established Judiciary Committee. Mansfield had to set up a Select Committee with the personnel of his own choosing. Had Mansfield lacked of determination to resolve this unjust campaign issue for his old friends, or, more importantly, had Sam Ervin not been there as a trustworthy old friend heading a Sub-Committee on Constitutional Rights and ready to take this job, or had Eastland been more determined and skillful in blocking the investigation, the struggle would have, at least, been prolonged.

Fortunately, Eastland did not pay much attention to this matter. He did not even reply to Mansfield's letter that suggested an investigation. Only after a few days when he met Mansfield on the Senate floor, Eastland lightly asked: "Got your letter, what do you want me to do?" "Give it over to Sam Ervin." Mansfield accomplished his first goal.[7]

A few days later, Mansfield met Ervin in the Senate Majority Leader's chambers. It was "a short, private, un-dramatic chat between two old friends." Mansfield recalled: "There was no need of us haranguing each other. I suggested a Select Committee, he agreed. . . . I told Sam I wanted no Democratic Presidential candidate on our side. This wasn't going to be a forum for a campaign. Sam agreed."[8]

Senator Sam Ervin of North Carolina played a crucial role thereafter. Although they shared the same conservative political views, Ervin and Nixon did not get along well. The personal relationship between Nixon and Ervin was rather cold. After the creation of the Senate Select Committee, Nixon called Ervin "one of four jackasses"—a favorite phrase Nixon used to use to call his enemies.[9] A month after the creation of the Ervin Committee, Nixon asked his aides to find a candidate to oppose Ervin in North Carolina and "nip at his heels."[10] This was not only due to Ervin being the Chairman of a committee to investigate him. One incident might be able to highlight the relationship between Ervin and Nixon several months before the creation of the Ervin Committee. Shortly after his re-election, Nixon had Ervin on his mind. He instructed Ehrlichman to make some move to embarrass Ervin for the benefit of Jesse Helms, Ervin's fellow North Carolinian in the Senate. Ehrlichman, by using Nixon's presidential power, fulfilled Nixon's wish. When Ervin asked Ehrlichman to waive a retirement-age requirement for a FCC commissioner, Ehrlichman coolly ignored him.[11] This kind of encounter would hardly nurture a positive interpersonal relationship between both parties involved.

On the contrary, Ervin had a good relationship with Senate Majority Leader Mike Mansfield. According to Ervin, Mansfield "is as fair and forthright a man as I have ever known."[12] They were "old friends" as Mansfield described.

But the key issue here was not about interpersonal relationships. Interpersonal relationships must be transformed into collective power. To accomplish this task, Mansfield must do everything in his power to ensure a fair appearance in the formalistic sense, i.e., such a Senate investigation must appear to be fair. The investigation itself was partisan enough. The fairness of the personnel and procedure of this investigation would be the only effective way to make it powerful enough to generate a collective power dynamic against Nixon's violation. As a consummate power player, Mansfield knew very clearly that such an investigation would be fraught with more political overtones than any other congressional investigation. The most powerful weapon for this purpose would be Sam Ervin as a person rather than the Senate as an institution.

Ervin was chosen based upon the reason that he "was 'the most nonpartisan Democrat' in the Senate;" and had never harbored any presidential or vice-presidential aspirations."[13] It would be very clear that the key here was to launch a collective process; only the person who had no presidential ambition could unify rather than polarize the powerful politicians in the Senate. Because he had a reputation of fair play, Ervin would be the most acceptable person interpersonally in the Senate for both parties to undertake such an investigation. Both the Republicans and Democrats in the Senate respected Ervin and he had been regarded as Richard Russell's heir apparent for leadership of the Democratic Southern caucus. The phrases they used to describe him like "integrity" "honesty" "fair-minded" were all highly subjective. However, these words at least showed that the interpersonal foundation that supported Ervin's efforts to launch a collective power process was solid. Here, the nature of the separation of powers and institutional checks and balances could be explained on the basis of mobilizing interpersonal resources for a collective effort. It was certain that Nixon could not control Ervin—either appointing him or dismissing him—institutionally. But he could make Ervin's life miserable if the latter was not powerful enough in the webs of interpersonal ties and his power was not rooted in collective power dynamics. With Patman, Nixon and his associates could amass sufficient power to defeat his investigation. But the collective power dynamics changed. With Ervin, they simply could not knock together enough powerful people to work for them. Few powerful politicians, both inside and outside Senate, would be willing to join Nixon's troops to attack Ervin. The White House tried to attack Ervin but the collective power was not in Nixon's favor. The social net Ervin wove over the years throughout his public careers in the collectivity of the political field was strong and his personal standing was solid. One incident can illustrate this point.

On May 17, 1973, the Charlotte, North Carolina, Observer carried an article reveal:

> The White House made an attempt two months ago to enlist North Carolina Republicans in a campaign to discredit Senator Sam J. Ervin, Jr., reliable sources have told the Observer. High officials in the North Carolina Republican Party confirmed Wednesday that H.R. "Bob" Haldeman, at that time President Nixon's Chief of Staff, made two attempts to get local party officials to "dig up something to discredit Ervin and blast him with it."[14]

Ervin himself stated this incident in this way: "Despite my lifelong allegiance to the Democratic Party, North Carolina Republicans have always treated me with great kindness. None of them attempted to dig up or disseminate anything to discredit me. On the contrary, one of the most distinguished of them, Charles R. Jonas, Jr., who had managed Nixon's campaign in North Carolina in 1968 and 1972, won my undying gratitude by paying me an exceedingly high compliment."[15] When he was interviewed in respect to the Observer article, Jonas stated:

> That would be an impossible task. I think that Senator Ervin is one of a handful of people in the Senate whom it would be impossible to discredit. I think that is why he was chosen. He has a record of impeccable honesty and integrity. If I had to depend on any one person in the Senate to proceed fairly and in a way that would protect the innocent, it would be Senator Ervin.[16]

Ervin's power, to a large extent, was deeply rooted in his social position in the political collectivity he had built with the powerful politicians in both parties both in Washington and back in North Carolina. Without such a substantive collective resource as his power base, Ervin's personal life would have been destroyed and his career would have been ruined before he even started to perform his institutional duty at all. Even if Nixon could not remove him institutionally, he could make his life miserable socially and politically before he could exercise his institutional role. Without strong and solid social support in the collective power dynamics, the checks and balances would become hollow. Therefore, Watergate was not a case of rational and institutional checks and balances that supported the "system worked" view. The collective power dynamics overwhelmed the formal institutional power. Also, it is important to make it explicit that the formal institutional construction meshed with informal interpersonal connections. The relationship between informal social networks and formal institutions was clear—the latter was embedded in the former.

While working behind-the-scenes to marshal Democratic support for the resolution, Mansfield kept Ervin in the forefront, relying on Ervin's social capital among Southern Democratic and Republican senators.

Meanwhile, Mansfield worked to secure a smooth proceeding.

On January 6, 1973, Mansfield called for a full investigation of Watergate, by a select committee armed with proper funds, staff, and subpoena powers. The time had come, Mansfield said, "to proceed to an inquiry into these matters in a dispassionate fashion." He shrewdly framed this issue as "constitutional." Mansfield declared, "At stake is the continued vitality of the electoral process."[17]

On January 11, Ervin formally accepted Mansfield's request that he preside over a thorough investigation of Watergate and the 1972 presidential campaign. The agreement signaled a powerful investigative web would be established on Capitol Hill beyond the preliminary inquiry Senator Kennedy's Judiciary Subcommittee on Administrative Practice and Procedure had been conducting.

On February 5, Senator Ervin introduced a resolution to create the Senate Select Committee on presidential campaign activities. It was clear that the target of the investigation would be the Watergate break-in and related allegations. Ervin proposed to allocate $500,000 for the investigation. The resolution called for a five-member committee, three Democrats and two Republicans, which would have the broadest powers to subpoena White House aides and probe fully into the Watergate bugging, its funding, planning, purpose and sponsorship.[18] It had been amended later to enlarge the committee to seven members, four Democrats and three Republicans, and to authorize the hiring of a minority counsel and staff to serve the minority members of the committee. The powerful Senate Democratic Policy Committee, which was under Mansfield's control, gave the resolution its support.

To Nixon, the Mansfield-Ervin alliance was too powerful to defeat. It represented a formidable collective power among powerful politicians in the high circle of Washington. Facing such a formidable power, the last-minute White House maneuver looked and proved very ineffective.

Before the floor debate, the White House, under the direction of Haldeman, tried to impede the process. A Republican aide told Woodward that the White House was "trying awfully hard," "word came down to make a big push." The White House source said to Woodward: " Haldeman's got half the staff here revved up on it. It's the order of the day. We're all supposed to make calls to people we know in the Senate."[19]

The party label here was not helpful to Nixon as it was in the Patman investigation. The revelation of Nixon's abuse of the commonly accepted codes among powerful politicians and his aggression against the political collectivity as a whole minimized the usual deep divisions and blatant partisanship. Party line only stirred up some stylized discourse. We heard more talks about declamations of noble purposes that were not necessarily reflecting the party line. We could see clearly the power of collective power dynamics. As a minority facing formidable collective power, the Republicans would make their decisions based on confirming to rather than opposing the collective purpose framed by Mansfield-Ervin alliance. Their amendments to the proposal for the Senate Select Committee focused on three counts.

The first Republican amendment was to broaden the investigation to include the '64 and '68 presidential campaign. Hugh Scott of Pennsylvania, the minority leader, led the charge that there was evidence of wiretapping against the Republicans in the 1968 campaigns. John Tower of Texas and Barry Goldwater of Arizona joined in, but no one offered a concrete example or made a specific charge.[20] Their purpose was only to show their "comradeship". They conformed to the collective purpose but tried to safeguard themselves by telling the other side "we are in the same boat" in case they pushed too hard. But in this case, the collective and dominate tone was to get the people who were directly responsible to the violations. This amendment was thus turned back.

The second was Senator Baker's amendment to increase the number of the Committee members to six and to divide the committee equally along partisan lines.[21] This amendment was in a purpose of seizing the procedure control in a party politics. However, it was voted down in a nearly party-line vote, 45-35.

The Republican's third amendment was only a face-saving gesture. They wanted one-third of the available funds to provide minority staffing. Ervin agreed to the proposal.

When the final vote was called, the Republicans joined their Democratic colleagues and the resolution passed unanimously, 77-0. This unanimity was rather a rare phenomenon from an institutional point of view. Unless there was a serious threat from the outside, it would be very difficult for the two party system to achieve such a high level unanimity. Clearly, Nixon was regarded as a serious outside threat to the high circle of powerful politicians. The power of the collective power dynamics revealed itself.

Baker, as the ranking Republican member on the Committee, and other Republican senators consistently applauded the idea of a Select Committee. To some Republican senators, what they said was more like gestures than convictions. Senator Jesse Helms probably expressed this Republicans' view more clearly: to them, the system worked pretty well so far. The FBI and the Patman investigations, and the media coverage, demonstrated that the Watergate situation had received enough scrutiny[22] and there was no surprise expected. However, this was, after all, a very serious issue and the collective power dynamics left very small space for them to maneuver. At this point, they would better choose to follow the majority.

The reason we say that the result did not reflect the senators' recognition of their institutional duty could also be seen from one scenario. If anyone other than Ervin had proposed this resolution, the same Senate institution might very well have directed their institutional duty to produce a different result. Had Kennedy, not Ervin, proposed Senate Resolution 60, the outcome would definitely have been different. Of the 77 U.S. Senators who voted for the resolution, most of them would fail to exhibit such a sense of institutional duty toward a "Kennedy Committee." Ervin was the only person who could deliver. It was because of his representation of the collective power. It would be clear that it was not the Senate as an institution or Ervin as a Senator that delivered this result. It was the power of the Mansfield-Ervin alliance and the collective power dynamics they skillfully developed that produced the unanimity. Certainly, if Ervin were not a Senator, he would not be able to play such a role. The Senate still had a formalistic function as a means for people to legitimize their action. All those Senators on the floor were sharp interpreters of the collective power dynamics. The formidable webs of interpersonal ties behind Ervin after Senator Mansfield's painstaking build-up since the election were a clear indication to the opponents of the resolution that Nixon was in deep trouble already. They needed to reconsider their best interest before they made any move. Although the high ground of Constitutionality only provided a cover for the whole maneuver, in a situation like this, the safest way would be to stand on a high ground—Constitutionality was the highest ground to stand.

The internal structure of the Ervin Committee also reflected the power represented by Senator Ervin. As a prime force in establishing the committee, Ervin also easily dominated it. At first glance, it seemed a lackluster committee. Except Senator Talmadge, Senators Inouye, Montoya, Baker, Gurney and Weicker were little known nationally and were not leaders in the Senate. It appeared strange that what was being called the most important investigation ever to be undertaken by the Senate was being entrusted largely to senators with little national reputation or influence. This was no accident, but was part of Ervin's intentional construction of his power within the Committee. His strategy was shared by Senator Mike Mansfield. With this Democratic set-up, Ervin could have the absolute authority without having to worry about being in a minority position. His Democratic colleagues gave him free rein. All three Democrats joined in unswerving support of Senator Ervin. Because of this set-up, his authority in the committee was never in jeopardy.

As to the three Republican members, only one, Senator Gurney, was a known partisan. But his lack of skill in terms of defending Nixon made him less troublesome. Senator Weicker was a freshman senator with little influence both in the Senate and across the nation. Senator Baker, the ranking minority member of the committee, was known as foxy. He was too clever to openly resist the overwhelming collective power of Ervin in the Committee. In fact, he eagerly gave an impression that he would not play a partisan role. These Republican Senators also had different reasons for serving on the committee. It was clear that Baker regarded the committee membership as a stepping stone for his Senate and national ambitions. Edward Gurney and Lowell Weicker actively campaigned to be on the committee. Weicker reportedly had been prepared to denounce the Republican leadership if he were denied a seat on the Senate Watergate Committee. Contrary to Gurney's loyalty to Nixon, Weicker was eager to go even one step further than the committee Democrats to expose Nixon's guilt. This Republican set-up determined that they were extremely weak as a partisan group and completely lacked the Democrats' cohesiveness. With no chance for unity, the Republicans on the Committee were clearly outnumbered and overwhelmed.[23]

THE IMMEDIATE IMPACT

The Republicans in the Senate had already started the uncoupling process between themselves and Nixon. Their strategy would be to separate Nixon from themselves as cleanly as possible. As long as they themselves could keep clean and they would not get harmed in the wave of the Washington collective power, those Republican politicians who were supposed to be on the Nixon side were ready to let Nixon take all the heat of his own making. If he could turn the collective power dynamics in his favor, he would be worth of their help; if Nixon could not make it, so be it. It was time to think about how to make the best of this newly developed collective power dynamics. Senator Baker's move after the vote on February 7 demonstrated this point.

After the vote, Senator Baker visited Tennessee and asked a former campaign worker, Fred Thompson, to serve as the Committee's Minority Counsel. It might be hard to make sense of why Baker chose Thompson for such an important job, especially compared to the Majority Council, Sam Dash. Thompson only had brief tenure as an Assistant U.S. Attorney in Tennessee with a few years in private practice, whereas Sam Dash was a man with a considerable background in criminal law as a prosecutor and professor. Dash, at forty-eight, was eighteen years older than Fred Thompson. His experience in the Philadelphia District Attorney's office and as a trial attorney in the Criminal Division of the Department of Justice, and his prominence in academic circles, clearly overwhelmed Thompson. Why did Baker choose to be simply overwhelmed? If we put his decision in context, we would be able to make sense of this move. A plausible explanation would be that Baker's intention was not defending the White House as best as he could do. He knew the power contest. The best way for him, not for Nixon, to make the best of the new situation would be to act independently without tying himself to a possible losing power. Therefore, what he needed was not an experienced criminal lawyer who could match Sam Dash. He only needed a man who would follow his orders without reservation. He did not need an independent mind but a controllable arm. Senator Baker understandably refused to accept White House guidance in appointing the minority counsel.

But shortly after his refusal of White House help, Baker requested a private, off-the-record meeting with Nixon. Nixon certainly wanted a soft-belly in the Senate Committee. According to Dean, Baker told the President that he did not want his contacts to be direct with the White House, and preferred to deal through Attorney General Richard Kleindienst as an intermediary. Nixon was satisfied with the meeting and confident that Baker would work for him inside the Committee.[24] If this were the case, the plausible interpretation would be that Baker was not so sure about his judgment about the collective power dynamics at that point and wanted to keep a back way retreat if something otherwise happened. But according to Baker, he only wanted to urge the President to give up his fighting on the issue of executive privilege. If we accept Baker's explanation, the plausible reasoning would be that Baker was convinced about the collective power dynamics and was sure that Nixon's only way out was to give up. His resistance would be useless except in dragging on the infighting. Such a situation would hurt every insider who was tied to Nixon. Whatever the case was, Baker started to play a role of double-dealing.

In sum, the supposed Nixon supporters in the Republican Party sensed the change of power. They stopped supporting him openly and started separating Nixon from themselves. They started making efforts to isolate Nixon from the interpersonal ties they shared before. Baker, with the appearance as a fair, nonpartisan person only pursuing the truth, served himself well in the end: a Republican, he nonetheless emerged from a Democratic-dominated show with his reputation substantially enhanced. He subsequently parlayed that performance into the position of Senate Republican leader and gained national visibility as a presidential contender.[25]

It is important to point out that the legal evidence gathered in the Watergate case did not increase much by that point. The evidence was still focused on the initial "Watergate Seven." Because of lack of evidence, Ervin skillfully maintained a correct posture toward Nixon. As Ervin made clear at the point when he accepted the chairmanship, he would be content if he could discover the role of

Magruder, John Mitchell's deputy in the CREEP.[26] At the outset, he declared it "simply inconceivable" that Nixon might have been involved. "I hope the Select Committee would be able to make a final report exonerating the President."[27]

However, the Committee's investigation started with three primary areas directly targeting the White House: the Watergate break-in and the cover-up; political espionage and campaign dirty tricks; and illegal campaign-financing practices. This was planned by Chief Counsel Sam Dash and was approved by Ervin. Each of the three Assistant Chief Counsels took one of these three areas.[28] It is important to be noted that although Ervin did not mention it explicitly, Dash's plan included cover-up as one of the three primary areas. The focus on cover-up fundamentally changed the nature of the investigation and directed the target at the White House and even Nixon. It would be too difficult, if not impossible, to find sound legal evidence beyond reasonable doubt that the high-ups in the Administration were involved in the break-in. On the contrary, the legal route would become clear if the investigation became focused on cover-up. Although the legal process basically stayed at where it was in the period between the Patman investigation and the Mansfield and Ervin resolution to create the Ervin Committee in the U.S. Senate, the transformation of the legal route completely shifted the investigation—it was not the evidence that changed the direction of investigation. It was the reframing of the Watergate case that dramatically reshaped the process.

Nixon knew the danger in this situation. He had successfully frustrated the Patman investigation. But this time his support was much thinner. The collective power dynamics had turned against him. Unlike the divided Patman Banking and Currency Committee, the Ervin Committee was fully prepared after several months' painstaking interpersonal networking led by Senator Mansfield and Ervin and it was unified under Ervin's firm control; even the whole Senate reached unanimity behind Ervin. The president's resources became comparatively limited, vulnerable, and ultimately, insufficient. Much of the post-election "mandate of American people" and the institutional expansion had started dismantling in the newly reshaped collective power dynamics; the sense of legitimacy after an overwhelming election victory had evaporated. Nixon warily glimpsed the future.

The press was a prime mover in the controversy only in terms of the Woodward and Bernstein investigation, which first linked the Watergate burglars to the Nixon campaign committee and, during the campaign, uncovered other stories that hinted at the politically explosive potential of the "bugging" incident. But with Nixon's decisive electoral victory, the press came close to abandoning Watergate. Then, as the issue revived and conflict over the scope of the investigation intensified, the press mainly lived off information that powerful politicians were happy to furnish. At first, the creation of the Senate Committee investigating Watergate still did not kindle much public interest. It did not even attract sufficient media attention. *The New York Times* covered the first day of the Senate debate on page 36; news of the resolution's passage moved up four pages.[29]

The Washington political leaders needed first to finish the formation of the collective power dynamics inside Washington before they pushed the outcome of their power struggle to the citizenry in general. So the first move would be attacking the Nixon camp in "a fair and legitimate" way.

THE GRAY HEARING

In the middle of the strong wave of the turn of the collective power dynamics among powerful politicians, especially in the Senate, the Gray nomination went to the wrong place—the Senate, at the wrong time—on February 17. It was Nixon's fateful and disastrous decision in this crucial period. Gray's confirmation hearings offered the already mobilized powerful politicians in Congress an immediate opportunity to raise questions about Watergate and became a congressional inquiry into the FBI's conduct of the Watergate investigation.

As the acting director of the FBI after J. Edgar Hoover's death, Gray helped Nixon put a lid on the Watergate break-in. But why did Nixon risk the possible consequences of a senatorial fishing expedition to make Gray's tenure permanent? Even the administration officials had a hard time making sense of this nomination. It was reported that there had been a debate in the innermost Nixon circle.[30] The only plausible explanation about this move could be: Nixon desperately tried to use his formal power through formal institutional channels to make up for his lack of power in the newly turned collective power dynamics.

Everybody knew that the FBI was in a position to play a key role in the cover-up. But the key factor here was that Gray was not Hoover. Nixon once expressed clearly that if Hoover were alive and directing the FBI, he would effectively put the Watergate affair to an end in time before it spread. In February 1973, just around the time Nixon sent Gray's name up for confirmation in the Senate, Nixon told John Dean that he was certain Hoover would have protected him. "He would have fought. That was the point. He would have defied a few people. He would have scared them to death. He had a file on everybody."[31] Nixon made it clear that he nostalgically yearned for the helping hands of Hoover. It was clear that the difference between Hoover and Gray was that Hoover painstakingly built up his own turf for decades. His formal power was deeply rooted in his informal interpersonal influence and control, which was more powerful in terms of the interpersonal power dynamics and had been well recognized both inside the FBI and outside it. Gray was new in this well knitted Hoover turf. It certainly took time to establish Gray's accepted authority through weaving his own interpersonal web of influence and control, even though he, like Hoover, was a comparable legitimate authority legitimately appointed by the President. Only after such a social and interpersonal construction could power transform itself into an accepted authority. Gray had not reached that point yet. But Nixon could not wait that long. His illegal activity was about to "blow up" and the Hoover style authority in the FBI was crucial to his survival. However, Gray's current authority status would not be strong enough to command those professional FBI agents to aid his cover-up action. As the duly formal authority, what Nixon could do at that point was only to make Gray's formal position permanent. Nixon might have wrongly hoped to accelerate Gray's informal authority-establishing process in a formal way. Gray was also wrong when he warned Nixon, according to Woodward, "all hell could break loose if he wasn't able to stay in the job permanently and keep the lid on."[32] For reason of misplacing formal authority with informal authority-establishing process, Nixon made a mistake and decided in a hurry to send Gray's name up to the Senate. Nixon, at this point, gravely miscalculated the strength and the determination of his adversaries.

Pat Gray's confirmation hearing was set to begin on February 28. His adversaries were already prepared to give him a hard time before the hearing. According to Bernstein and Woodward, the night before, Bernstein talked to Tom Hart, a young aide to Senator Robert Byrd of West Virginia. Byrd, as the Senate Democratic Whip and a member of the Judiciary Committee, was very powerful at the time. To prepare for the hearing, Hart had compiled a card index of the newspaper and magazine stories and, from these, had filled a loose-leaf binder with lists of contradictions and unanswered questions about Watergate. These questions were being circulated to selected members of the committee. Byrd was determined to get the answers for these questions. Even if the Judiciary Committee reported a positive recommendation, Byrd would use his considerable influence to oppose the nomination on the Senate floor if the contradictions were not cleared up.[33]

The hearings exposed the relationship between Gray and John Dean in the cover-up. While insisting that the Watergate investigation had been "a massive special" with "no holds barred," Gray revealed that he had turned over the files of the investigation to John Dean and was close to admitting that he had cooperated with Dean in seeking to limit the investigation to the break-in. John Dean, the coordinator of the entire cover-up conspiracy, was therefore exposed for the first time. The web of cover-up started disintegrating. It became clear that Dean would not be able to stay behind the stage any more. A Dean hearing was looming large after the Gray hearings.[34]

THE SIRICA FACTOR

After the creation of the Ervin Committee, politicians finished their first stage power struggle that turned the collective power dynamics against Nixon and his associates. They therefore shaped the general atmosphere and set up the stage for the court and the entire justice system to act. Their determination and strength of power provided both the sufficient and necessary pre-condition for the court and the entire criminal justice system to play its institutional role. To transform the case from a "third-rate burglary" to "the highest level cover-up," it was necessary for legitimized criminal justice system to finish the job legally. The legal battle began with the court trial of the seven Watergate defendants.

The sitting Judge for this case was John Sirica. He played an active role in the trial. According to him, it was the independence of the judiciary system that made it possible for him to play such a role and eventually broke the case. "The basic strength of our system of government is tied to the continuing independence of the judicial system from political and social pressures. As a trial judge, I found that the greatest pleasure I derived from my work was that very independence."[35]

How could we understand the "independence" of the judiciary system? How could we understand the role Sirica played in the Watergate trial?

First of all, the judiciary system is by no means independent. Clearly, if we regard the judiciary system as an objective structure, we might overlook the fundamental nature of the system, which is, by nature, interpersonal and collective. The formal structure is embedded in the informal social relationships and socially constructed collective dynamics. Sirica's own journey to the federal bench best demonstrated this point. Sirica started his political career by working in the two Eisenhower elections. In this way, he made the friends who finally helped him get on the bench. One of these friends was Leonard Hall who later became Republican National Committee chairman. Sirica expressed to him his desire to be a federal judge. Opportunity finally came.

In the fall of 1956, a District Court judge retired. Sirica was then serving on the Republican State Committee for the District. So he got Len Hall to support him in the White House. William Rogers, whom Sirica had known for a long time, was then deputy attorney general. One of his duties was as screener of judicial nominees. Rogers was one of Sirica's strongest supporters. As Sirica stated clearly: "I'm sure now that without his help, I would not have received the appointment to the federal bench. Ever since, I have been most grateful to Rogers and the others who were in my corner when I was seeking the judgeship."[36]

It was the interpersonal affiliation that penetrated the judiciary system from the very beginning in a fundamental way. It was certain that, institutionally, Sirica could not be fired, threatened, or otherwise disciplined by a Republican president or anyone. However, the web of interpersonal ties would be able to ruin his career and to make his life miserable if he somehow violated the code in this interpersonal web. The system could protect him from institutional threat but he had to follow the interpersonally constructed codes within his web of interpersonal ties.

Secondly, what does a party affiliation mean? We all know that the American party system is not a rigid formal organization. Party discipline is weak and party members are not bound so tightly. Parties as a whole are not so well organized and solidified. In Sirica's case, we can see this point clearly. Although he was a Republican, he had no organizational obligation to the Republican Party. His binding to the party was rather interpersonal. It was only because he had some friends who happened to be Republicans and who had helped him along the way of his career advancement, also, it was because Sirica felt comfortable being with them that he became a Republican and stayed that way.

Sirica himself admitted that his loyalty to the Republican Party was originated and maintained by interpersonal ties to his friends. He stated his party affiliation this way:

> The Republicans had done me a favor. I never forgot it. It's hard to say whether my political views were conservative before I got that job through the Republicans or whether they became conservative because of the association, but in any event it was the start of a long relationship.[37]
>
> Like many lawyers, I found that politics became a sort of hobby. I never thought of seeking elective office, but after the Republicans helped me get into the U.S. attorney's office, I wanted to help them out in return. I didn't want them to think I was ungrateful. My father was a red-hot Democrat. He disliked Herbert Hoover with a passion and couldn't understand how I could be a Republican. But most of my friends were Republicans and I felt comfortable there.[38]

The interpersonal affiliation with the Republican Party determined that Sirica would be more influenced by his close friends and colleagues than by the Party as an organization. The process of assigning the case to himself revealed this aspect of the judiciary system.

In an account, Sirica said he took the case only because of his party identity as a Republican so that when a potential conflict came up, he could be right in the middle. But, an interesting question might be: Why didn't he worry at all about the obvious risk for a Republican Judge perceived as favoring a Republican administration or a Republican president? It did not make sense to conclude that it was the rational and political consideration that determined the case-assignment process. As Sirica described, all the people whom he had asked about the case-assignment were his friends with whom he felt comfortable. Some of them were Democrats, some of them were Republicans, but they were all good friends. It was exactly the informal friend circle that decided the process.[39]

Rather, Republican or Democrat was just a label here. The case-assignment process, with its political or legal tone, was more like a process of constructing interpersonal relations through certain socially accepted dynamics, rather than a formal legal procedure. It was not objectively following the law. From the very beginning, for Sirica and for all the people he consulted about this matter, political consideration was a factor, but the interpersonal dynamics in a web of comfortable interpersonal relationships were more decisive.

This aspect of the Sirica phenomenon led us to the third aspect, that is, the Sirica phenomenon reflected the fact that Sirica's personal conviction about law and order was rather socially constructed by his position in the interpersonal ties he had been making living from. It reflected distinctively about Sirica as a member of an interpersonal network, a friend circle with all the people in it holding similar philosophy about dealing with legal matters. Such an interpersonally constructed legal philosophy, more than the judiciary system as a whole, basically shaped Sirica's drive for a tough trial.

Sirica personally liked Nixon before 1973.[40] However, with the nick name as "maximum John," Sirica was a tough sentencer, which brought him reputation and influence in his interpersonal web. It was clear that Sirica's active role in the trial had more to do with his believing in "law and order" and tough sentencing than to his commitment to his institutional duty as a judge. He liked the slogan of "law and order," which was also advocated by most of his Republican friends, as well as Nixon himself. It was very ironic that Sirica was carrying out Nixon's policy and the very Republican philosophy in a legal atmosphere that most of Sirica's friends, and by Nixon himself, strove to create. It was clear that the Sirica factor highlighted the Washington collective power dynamics in the high political circle.

NOTES

1. Kutler, Stanley I. *The Wars of Watergate: The Last Crisis of Richard Nixon.* (New York: Knopf, 1990), 255.

2. White, Theodore. *Breach of Faith: The Fall of Richard Nixon.* (New York: Atheneum, 1975), 229–230.

3. Ervin, Sam Jr. *The Whole Truth: The Watergate Conspiracy.* (New York: Random House, 1980), viii-ix.
4. Bernstein, Carl and Bob Woodward. *All the President's Men.* (New York: Simon & Schuster, 1974), 247.
5. White, *Breach of Faith,* 230.
6. Woodward, Bob and Carl Bernstein. *The Final Days.* (New York: Simon & Schuster, 1976), 178.
7. White, *Breach of Faith,* 230.
8. White, *Breach of Faith,* 231.
9. Kutler, *The Wars of Watergate,* 345.
10. Kutler, *The Wars of Watergate,* 257.
11. Kutler, *The Wars of Watergate,* 345.
12. Ervin, *The Whole Truth,* viii-ix.
13. Ervin, *The Whole Truth,* ix.
14. Ervin, *The Whole Truth,* 25.
15. Ervin, *The Whole Truth,* 25.
16. Ervin, *The Whole Truth,* 25-26.
17. Kutler, *The Wars of Watergate,* 252.
18. Dash, Samuel. *Chief Counsel: Inside the Ervin Committee.* (New York: Random House, 1976), 8.
19. Bernstein and Woodward. *All the President's Men,* 250.
20. Bernstein and Woodward. *All the President's Men,* 250.
21. Dash, *Chief Counsel,* 9.
22. Kutler, *The Wars of Watergate,* 257.
23. Kutler, *The Wars of Watergate,* 344; Dash, *Chief Counsel,* 9-10.
24. Dean, John W. III. *Blind Ambition: The White House Years.* (New York: Simon & Shuster, 1976), 322.
25. Kutler, *The Wars of Watergate,* 345; Dash, *Chief Counsel,* 112-114; 153-155.
26. Bernstein and Woodward. *All the President's Men,* 249.
27. Ervin, *The Whole Truth,* 19.
28. Dash, *Chief Counsel,* 21.
29. Kutler, *The Wars of Watergate,* 257.
30. Bernstein and Woodward. *All the President's Men,* 269-270.
31. Kutler, *The Wars of Watergate,* 101.
32. Bernstein and Woodward. *All the President's Men,* 270.
33. Bernstein and Woodward. *All the President's Men,* 217-272.
34. Bernstein and Woodward. *All the President's Men,* 272.
35. Sirica, John J. *To Set the Record Straight: The Break-in, the Tapes, the Conspirators, the Pardon.* (New York: Norton, 1979), 127.
36. Sirica, *To Set the Record Straight,* 38-39.
37. Sirica, *To Set the Record Straight,* 33-34.
38. Sirica, *To Set the Record Straight,* 36.
39. Sirica, *To Set the Record Straight,* 48-50.
40. Kutler, *The Wars of Watergate,* 260.

Chapter Three

The Strength of the Washington Collective Power

THE WATERGATE BURGLARY TRIAL

The trial of Hunt, Liddy, and the Watergate burglars began on January 10 in the U.S. District Court for the District of Columbia. Assistant U.S. Attorney Earl Silbert made it clear that this case was about the break-in. Although he mentioned that the break-in was a part of a well-financed, many-layered espionage and "special intelligence" operation against the Democratic Party, and he also finger-pointed the Committee to Re-elect the President as the organizer of all these illegal behaviors, Silbert and his assistants had confined the case narrowly. He only promised to offer evidence on the recruitment of spies, earlier attempts to bug McGovern's offices, the monitoring of telephone calls from the tap in the Democrats' Watergate headquarters, and the other related activities of Watergate five and Hunt and Liddy. The defendants had been indicted on multiple counts of burglary, conspiracy, and interception of wire and oral communications. For the quality of prosecuting, Silbert framed his indictment with "shrewd parsimony," restricting himself to those offenses that appeared beyond dispute. Especially in a situation that in other matters the liberal Circuit Court of Appeals had reversed decisions of presiding Judge "Maximum John" Sirica to an unusual degree, the prosecutors had reason to do so. But their indictment added nothing to the cover-up case.[1]

On January 30, after deliberating only ninety minutes, the jury returned guilty verdicts on charges against McCord and Liddy. It seemed that Sirica expanded the scope of Watergate from break-in to cover-up in his court. But the role Sirica actually played was limited. He made it clear that what he had done had contributed to breaking the Watergate case. As he asserted: "by late March, with the trial over, there didn't seem a lot more I could do about it."[2]

It is important to note that the success of his active interference in the trial had more to do with the overall collective power dynamics than to the independence of the judiciary system. The judiciary system was, to some extent, insulated from political interference—the President could not do anything institutionally and formally to Sirica if the latter chose to do something. But the power within Sirica's reach was limited. He could only play a relatively active role, which was tough sentencing to force a defection.

Sirica only reflected the entire atmosphere in Washington. He could not achieve what he had achieved without those powerful politicians who had already shaped the entire political and legal environment. As he wrote: "I was far from alone in my skepticism about the facts brought out at the trial. The Senate of the United States had voted to investigate the Republican campaign tactics. The press was full of caustic comment about the trial itself and the government's handling of it."[3] Sirica's statement reflected that he felt the power and strength of the parallel developments in Washington. The Gray hearing was underway in the Senate and some revelations started emerging. The Ervin Committee and its investigation put enormous pressure on the Justice Department's prosecutors: if they didn't want to end up looking like fools or worse, they had better go along with the Washington collective power. The prosecutors were certainly not fools. They were very sensitive to the collective power dynamics in Washington where they lived and made a living and acquired fame. They therefore appeared very active and dynamic in the trial. They assured Sirica they would bring the burglars back before the grand jury, after their sentencing, for additional grilling.

The Senate Watergate Committee was the driving force at this crucial point.

Sam Dash, an experienced prosecutor, observed, after he took the position as the majority counsel of the Ervin Committee:

> I had no doubt that our investigation was confronting a major cover-up conspiracy. It seemed obvious we would need the help of an insider—an informer to successfully expose this conspiracy. Some extraordinary tactic had to be employed to induce one or more of the burglars to start talking."[4]

According to Sam Dash, he and Sirica had been friends for years as faculty colleagues at Georgetown University Law Center. Although he did not recommend anything regarding the sentencing of the Watergate defendants, he expressed the hope that one of them might give invaluable information about the cover-up. Both Dash and Sirica knew that the only way to unravel the cover-up would be to have an insider to start talking. Judge Sirica responded that he would use his power to serve the interests of justice in the sphere the law allowed. Here, the court got empowered by the collective power already mobilized in the high political circle. The two forces started converging.[5]

Congressman Wright Patman did not stay idle, either. Henry Petersen, still in charge of the Watergate investigation, assured him that his office had closely followed the leads provided by Patman's staff. He made it clear that attorneys in the Justice Department under his leadership were "vigorously " pursuing "all evidentiary leads." That same day, the Justice Department filed charges against CREEP for campaign-financing violation.[6]

The screw was tightening in the circle of the professional bureaucrats after the mobilization of the collective power dynamics among powerful politicians. They were going to produce something under the tightening scrutiny of the powerful politicians. But it was still too early for the ordinary citizens to get interested in this Watergate saga. Despite Judge Sirica's dramatic attempts to uncover bigger news, the verdict in the Watergate trial made little news. When the trial began, reporters treated it as no more than a commonplace criminal event. Newspapers like *The New York Times* placed it in the inside pages. Howard Hunt's guilty plea made the headlines only briefly before attention waned quickly. The lack of attention in the mass media reflected the lack of interest of the public in the wake of Nixon's overwhelming triumph.[7] The mobilized collective power dynamics had not gone beyond the powerful politician and high-level state bureaucrats.

BREAKING MCCORD

McCord's defection marked a major break-through in the case in the legal sense. The breaking of McCord, one of the Watergate burglars, reflected the joint power of the mobilized political force and the judiciary one. Shortly after the creation of the Ervin Committee, its mighty power became apparent. McCord's lawyer Fensterwald soon found Dash. He told him that he was confident he could produce McCord for Dash as a witness.

According to Dash, McCord was suspicious of the U.S. attorney's office. He believed that since both the U.S. attorney's office and the FBI were in the chain of command to the White House, he couldn't trust these two agencies. "The integrity of the system would not be preserved."[8]

Dash soon made a note to alert Judge Sirica about McCord's fears concerning the government agencies and the legal procedures. The mobilized personal connections worked together here to break the case. A few days later, on March 21, Judge Sirica called Dash to inform him of his sentencing of the Watergate defendants on March 23: "I think you should be present in the courtroom when I sentence them. What I plan to do should be of special interest to you and the committee."[9]

It turned out that the day of sentencing was a very important day that transformed the break-in into cover-up in the judiciary line of investigation.

Three days before the sentencing day, James McCord delivered a letter to Judge Sirica that led directly to the unraveling of the conspiracy. McCord told Sirica that there had been pressure to force the defendants maintain silence; that many people perjured themselves in the trial; that he knew that many government officials, none of them CIA agents, were involved in Watergate. McCord told the Judge that he wanted an opportunity to discuss the case at greater length with him.

After reading McCord's letter in court on March 23, Judge Sirica turned to the sentencing of the other defendants. He was convinced that he could use his power to force cooperation from the defendants. Sirica believed that McCord's letter and his own actions vitally affected events. "The fact that despite his fears about the Justice Department and even the prosecutors, McCord sensed that he could trust the court, and would be protected by them, changed the course of the Watergate case."[10] Sirica thought that McCord's "trust" in him and the courts led to the letter.[11] This was certainly a part of the case. But it was certainly partial.

Sirica overlooked the general context and the greater forces around both himself and McCord. McCord' lawyer had contacted Dash before and the Senate's investigators had begun to approach similar leads. McCord did not rely on Sirica alone for his defection. He hadn't fully trusted Sirica and had given Bob Jackson, of the Los Angeles Times, a copy of the letter in return for a promise to print it if no action was taken by Sirica. Clearly, McCord's defection that blew the case wide open was only possible after the convergence of so many forces working together. Without an extra guarantee, McCord would not risk a confrontation with the entire Nixon troops. Sirica alone, although backed by the "independent" judiciary system, could not get the trust of those insiders like McCord who knew the issue of omnipresent power in the system. In fact, the Gray hearings in late February and still underway by that time had already revealed the cover-up conspiracy. In addition, the prosecutors were still pressuring on this case. They tried to induce the Watergate defendants to cooperate. But, still the letter sent to Sirica was very important in terms of propelling the case in the direction of discovering the cover-up. The day after McCord sent his letter to Sirica, Dean told Nixon that there was "a cancer on the presidency." All the insiders knew that the case, to use a favorite Oval Office expression, was about to blow.

McCord prepared a brief memorandum and sent it to Dash to support the perjury charge he had made in his letter to Judge Sirica. Dash was shocked by the naked assertions in the memorandum. The charges here provided a solid base for the Senate Committee to act on information, rather than suspicion. The role of G. Gordon Liddy was revealed in the memorandum that he was only a subordinate in the Watergate burglary. Further more, Jeb Magruder was involved in the break-in and had lied in his testimony. McCord also exposed

John Dean's involvement. Clearly, in addition to Gray's revelation, McCord's letter and memorandum led the investigation further on the road of uncovering the cover-up.[12]

But the politicians on the Senate Committee reacted to the McCord revelation differently than the legal professionals did. They were eager to involve themselves in the case but reacted cautiously to all McCord's allegations. They faced a much larger and more complicated task than simply dealing with legal evidence. To maintain the strength of the collective power dynamics, they had to deal with a variety of forces with different strengths of power on all sides of the struggle; they had to mobilize their troops and unify their hard core; they had to project a favorite image both in front of the public and among themselves in order not to give their adversaries any chance to enhance their power. In a word, they needed to work on the power dynamics slowly but solidly. The Committee at its meeting on March 27 voted to hear McCord's testimony.

In the private hearing before the full Committee, McCord expected to be embraced by the Committee as a witness. After all, he had voluntarily come forward with inside information. However, he found himself subjected to rather hostile cross-examination. Senator Talmadge snapped a series of short, sharp questions to McCord. Other Senators joined in. Together, they reduced McCord's testimony about Mitchell, Dean and Magruder to bare hearsay. At Baker's recommendation, the committee rejected McCord's request for immunity.[13]

Judge Sirica again postponed McCord's sentencing. He suggested to McCord that he finish his testimony to the Senate Committee first, then to complete his testimony to the grand jury. The Senate Committee might have scored some political points by trying to consolidate McCord's shocking allegations and refusing to immunize him for the time being, but it lost legal points this time. McCord's lawyer went directly to the prosecutors to seek immunity for McCord after the Senate Committee had refused it to him. McCord was in a situation in which he must tell everything he knew to an official body as soon as possible in order to get himself disentangled from all the legal difficulties. He went to Judge Sirica first, who only had limited power; then he went to the Senate Committee but it refused his request. His last choice was the grand jury and the U.S. attorney's office which he distrusted before. But he got what he needed there. Sirica granted McCord immunity at Silbert's request.[14]

Only because he had so many choices when he wanted to break silence, did McCord get the opportunity to come out and reveal what he knew. The collective power dynamics at this point showed their significance.

Meanwhile, the evidence corroborating process went forward nicely in the Senate Committee. McCord's hearsay accounts of the roles of Mitchell, Dean and Magruder in Liddy's political bugging activities got corroboration. Magruder's former appointment secretary, Robert Reisner, Vicky Chern, and Liddy's former secretaries, Sylvia Panarites and Sally Harmony, were interviewed by the Committee staff. They corroborated the major stories in McCord's allegation; Vicky Chern's diary book provided solid documentary evidence.

Magruder told Sam Dash later that he knew everything would come out when he learned that Reisner was subpoenaed by the Senate Committee.[15] The Senate Committee gained both political points and legal points by this time.

Still, to this point, the citizens in general were not involved. The creation of the Senate Select Committee itself had caused barely a ripple of public attention. It was not only because the change was too rapid and the revelations were too dramatic, but also because the collective power dynamics were still limited in the high political circle. Reporters waited until near the end of the President' March 2nd press conference to raise a rather polite Watergate question.[16]

With the revelations eventually unveiled in the Gray hearings and the chain of effects resulting from McCord's defection, "Watergate" rapidly became a meaningful—and loaded—political term that spread across the press, raising far-reaching political concerns. "During March, White House reporters posed 478 questions to Press Secretary Ron Ziegler. The trickle of Watergate news in March swelled into a rampaging stream."[17]

Woodward and Bernstein wrote, with excitement, about the events after McCord's revelation: "Much bigger forces were firmly in charge. Government investigations were under way, and the instinct for survival could turn some of the President's men into informers."[18] Indeed, those bigger forces, mentioned by Woodward and Bernstein, were firmly in charge.

THE DEAN DEFECTION

Clearly, Dean, as the ringmaster of the cover-up, was the key. Dean's defection would be the strongest stream in the flood that would sweep away Haldeman, Ehrlichman, and, even the President.

On March 29, Magruder learned that the Senate Committee had served a subpoena on Reisner, and he tried his last resource. If all the participants in the meetings that planned the break-in stuck to the false story about the content of those meetings, there might be a hope that the cover-up might be able to continue. At the meeting with Mitchell and Dean at the White House, Magruder tried to obtain the other two's assurance about the false story if they were called as witnesses before the Senate Committee or the Watergate grand jury. But Dean, knowing how desperate Magruder was and how serious the situation was, had already lost faith in the cover-up. To be forced to testify before the Senate committee or the grand jury would be a serious business, he would have no choice but to tell the truth under the current circumstances. He told Magruder that he would reveal what had been discussed at both the January and February meetings in Mitchell's office.[19]

This clash of former conspirators was clearly pressed by the powerful forces of Senate Committee, the court and the U.S. Attorney's office in the Justice Department. The government agencies had been transformed into an investigative web after those powerful politicians successfully developed the collective power dynamics against Nixon and therefore transformed the issue from break-in to cover-up. The creation of the Senate Watergate Committee energized and reinforced the court and the U.S. attorneys in the executive branch. They were working on the same target at the same time while mutually stimulating and mutually checking.

Sam Ervin made it clear that he would challenge the President's claims of executive privilege. He was trying to make sure that he would gain the testimony of key White House aides; the Senate investigation widened in scope. If the executive privilege became a non-issue, Nixon's subordinates would lose the last protection. They would be forced to become potential witnesses. Under the severe potential punishment by law, they had little choice but to tell the truth under oath.[20]

As a government agency, the U.S. Attorney's office was subjected to the control of the dominant political power in the government. As the Watergate case was transformed from break-in to cover-up after the New Year of 1973, the prosecutors did their job pretty well. McCord's revelation and the subsequent investigations had shown the strength of the government forces. By mid-April before Nixon's April 17 announcement, the U.S. Attorney's office had discovered the Plumbers' operations, and gained several guilty pleas. They had broken Magruder. Jeb Magruder had readily accepted Silbert's deal of pleading guilty to one count of obstructing justice and become the prosecutors' witness. The prosecutors had also gained Dean's partial and half-hearted cooperation, without granting him immunity. Based upon their testimony, the prosecutors had found reliable evidence to uncover the existence of a massive conspiracy to obstruct justice that involved several of Nixon's close aides, including Haldeman, Ehrlichman, and Dean, among others. The prosecutors informed Assistant Attorney General Petersen that they were on the verge of indicting these people for their roles in the break-in and the cover-up. Some attorneys even started to suspect Nixon with sound evidence.[21]

Meanwhile, the Senate Committee had already pointed its investigation directly to Nixon. As Thompson, the minority counsel, described: by April 25, both Dean and Magruder had implicated Nixon before Dash. On the night of April 25, Thompson wrote in his journal: "The focus is on the president now. The word 'impeachment' is beginning to creep into Capitol Hill conversation. A Gallup poll shows that about a third of the American people believe he 'knew.' Many believe the entire White House staff will go. The key issue is now crystallized: when did the president first know? Presumably after the break-in."[22]

Dean was the crucial link in the chain of cover-up that would lead to Nixon. For Dean, the possibility to choose among these powerful forces was the crucial factor for him in his decision to go forward. A relative low-profile judicial approach in Judge John Sirica's court had still not gotten very far with its criminal investigation of the cover-up. Sirica had to take his time and think long and hard on the majesty of the law. He could not give Dean what he wanted—the immunity.[23]

For getting immunity from the prosecutors, Dean had confined his incriminating remarks on Haldeman and Ehrlichman and later decided to implicate Nixon as well. But Silbert stood fast, because he did not want both Dean and the prosecution to suffer a loss of credibility. He also firmly believed that Dean was the ringmaster of the cover-up, the very one who ought to get the punishment he deserved.[24]

Dean had a very complicated relationship with the U.S. Attorney's office. According to him, the major issue was trust. He suspected that the prosecutors might merely claim triumph for having broken him and then find insufficient evidence for other cases. He and his lawyer both inclined not to cast their lot with them.[25]

Silbert took Dean before the grand jury, hoping to force Dean to tell his story under oath. But Dean pleaded his Fifth Amendment privilege. For the moment, Dean started openly confronting the prosecutors. He chose to cooperate completely with the Senate Committee. He saw that to go to the Senate Committee would give him opportunity to talk to the public in the public hearings. That would give him the best forum to get his story out—and consequently to win him public support. This, in turn, would be used as leverage for a better deal with the prosecutor.[26]

According to Dean, his two lawyers had leaned toward the Senate committee from the beginning. The most important reason was that Dean needed a strong collective power to back him up. This power must be able to give him a chance to pump up the credibility that was vitally important for Dean as a subordinate to accuse the President of the United States. Two other reasons were: first, McCandless, one of his two lawyers, had a string of contacts in the Senate and he could help behind the scenes—lots of maneuvering would go on off camera; third, the use immunity the Senate would give Dean would make it more difficult to prosecute Dean, if it not impossible. The law requires that the testimony under use immunity cannot be used against the defendant. The prosecutors have to prove they got none of their evidence from the defendant's testimony. Also, by playing the Senate against the prosecutors, Dean would be able to increase his chance of getting total immunity from the prosecutors.[27]

Meanwhile, the Senate Committee was debating about whether to give Dean use immunity. At its May 8 meeting, Senator Baker was against any immunity for Dean. His reason was similar to that of the prosecutors, that was, although Dean could be a key witness, he was also the most culpable and dangerous person in the Watergate affair. Therefore, he did not want to risk the public criticism for offering Dean immunity when the U.S. attorney's office had rejected this deal.[28] His position was very clear. In the power game, he needed to consolidate his position in the collective power dynamics. Coming from the same camp, he and Nixon still had countless ties in terms of their power bases. Before this power base as a whole was ready to abandon Nixon, Baker would skillfully play safe. At the same time, he realized the new direction of the newly developed collective power dynamics. Nixon's power base was bound to abandon him. More and more of his supporters had lost their intention to engage in a bloody battle for saving Nixon. They would have too many casualties in such a battle and it was not worth it. It would take time for most of the people in that camp to recognize this situation but it was only a matter of time. Baker knew this. The only thing he needed to do was to handle the timing well. Therefore, at that point, what he did was to present a fair and bi-partisan image in front of the public in order to lead the event in certain directions while slowing the pace of attacking Nixon to a degree that was correspondent with the reaction of his and Nixon's same power base. His fine line "What did the President know and when did he know it," clearly represented this strategy.

But his Republican colleague Weicker was not so skillful. Unlike Baker, he seemed not to care about how much influence and power he would lose in the Republican camp by being out front in the investigation. He focused on pre-empting the Democrats by rushing one step ahead of them. As an institutional player, he played his institutional role quite faithfully and functionally; but he was seen as a deviant, too abnormal for his fellow senators to understand. Both Republicans and Democrats regarded him as an over-zealous freshman, trying to establish his own reputation. Some of them even thought that he just wanted to get revenge on Nixon for his friend Pat Gray.[29]

With the support of Weicker, Ervin knew his power would surely overwhelm. Therefore, he immediately moved that the Committee approve that a subpoena be issued to John W. Dean, III, and that the Committee agree to grant Dean use immunity.[30]

Senator Ervin's motion would be approved by the required two-third vote even though Baker and his Republican colleague, Senator Gurney, who was absent, objected. As clever as Baker was, he immediately said that he would follow the majority of the Committee. The reason was, as he explained, that he was concerned about the Committee's public image and Committee unanimity would result in greater public confidence in the committee's work. But, at the same time, he wanted the record to show that he had grave concern about asking for immunity for Dean at this time.[31]

Behind the three government investigation arms, there were strong collective power dynamics. If John Dean did not have much more powerful political allies, his defection would not happen, or at least, would not be so complete. He might only reveal the role of Haldeman and Ehrlichman and would never mention "Mr. P" [Nixon]. As McQuaid pointed out: "How all this happened was not a saga of innate republican virtue. Political people made political decisions based on political calculations. Growing numbers of, above all, pragmatic political survivors began to equate their best interest with a struggle with the White House."[32]

AS THE COLLECTIVE POWER DYNAMICS TURNED

From March on, critics from both parties dominated congressional commentary. Powerful liberal Democrats—notably, senators Muskie, McGovern, and Fulbright—exploited the wider opportunities by warning of the dangers of dictatorship. McGovern had made such charges during his unsuccessful presidential bid; now he and others were listened to, and not by Democrats alone. They thought they could benefit from advocating legislative reforms. Even many congressional moderates and some conservatives sensed the power shift and started to separate themselves from Nixon as the Watergate situation intensified from March to May 1973.[33] They realized that Watergate was an essential power struggle. It was both threatening and benefiting for a far broader circle of powerful people depending on how they dealt with this new situation. The process of uncoupling began. Under strong collective power dynamics, more and more moderate Republicans had started to express their opinion with a morally and politically correct tone. Minority Leader Hugh Scott of Pennsylvinia complained that he was "deeply disturbed." Senator Marlow Cook of Kentucky pointedly raised the concern about the relationship between Nixon and the Republican Party. He said that the whole affair cast a "severe stigma on the Republican Party."[34]

The conservative forces, even the most conservative faction in the Republican Party, were not necessarily the ones whose interests were threatened by the investigation. On the contrary, they separated themselves from Nixon and projected an image as the true representative of the authority system as a whole in a timely fashion. On March 27, three leading conservative Republican senators, James Buckley of New York, Norris Cotton of New Hampshire, and John Tower of Texas, demanded that Nixon and Dean speak out and clarify matters.[35]

Even Goldwater, the most conservative Senator, started to change. At first, the Watergate scandal itself had little impact on Goldwater's attitude toward Nixon. Democratic allegations of Republican "dirty tricks" did not bother Goldwater at all. He flatly dismissed the Watergate break-in as an isolated incident, and regarded it as "unimportant" and politics as usual. However, as more and more powerful politicians, ranging from the liberal Democrats to many moderates and even some conservatives, joined the collective force, Goldwater started to turn around. As "comrades", colleagues and "friends" for so many years working, fighting, and campaigning together, the leaders of the conservative camp knew Nixon better than anyone else. Most of them privately entertained doubts about the president's integrity for a long time. Now at this juncture, they were more certain than others about Nixon's involvement in a major cover-up. "This," said Senator John Tower, "was not necessarily untypical of Nixon. He just thought he could get away with it." Barry Goldwater, too, had stories to tell. At the "Munich of the Republican Party," the 1960 convention, he called Nixon "a two-fisted, four-square liar." Nixon's overweening ambition during the 1964 campaign had also exposed serious character flaws.[36] This series of personal experiences would help Goldwater and other conservative politicians assimilate new evidence and discern the pattern of duplicity and wrongdoing. It was not the evidence revealed by the legal process that pushed these conservative leaders to separate themselves from Nixon. It was the collective power dynamics that made them feel the necessity for them to do so. But they did this slowly, gradually, and skillfully.

Goldwater restated his faith in the president but noted, "I might not support him if it turns out he knew all about this and kept his mouth shut."[37] Yet at the same time, Goldwater consistently advised Richard Nixon "to come clean, lay the whole thing on the table, tell everything about it that [you] had not told the people and everything would be all right." In April 1973, when the situation became more severe, Goldwater put on a face as a moral authority and made a public plea. He told the *Christian Science Monitor* that the crisis demanded that Richard Nixon come forward and give "assurances" to the American people. "The Watergate. The Watergate. It's beginning to be like Teapot Dome."[38]

George McGovern also used Teapot Dome as an analogy to frame Watergate in his 1972 presidential champion. It was so uncharacteristic to hear these words from Goldwater.

THE "APRIL 30TH EXPLOSION" AND THE NIXON PRESIDENCY ON ITS DEATHBED

After the creation of the Ervin Committee in the Senate, the growing evidence started to show that Watergate was not an anomaly but a small piece of a larger pattern of Nixon administration's illegal activities. The persistent probe yielded startling revelations of Nixon and his close associates' damaging behavior. As Nixon lost more and more power, the possibility of White House complicity became more and more clear. Nixon became more and more entangled in this mess without much power to get out of it. All became clear on April 16th, 1973.

After talking to Petersen, who was in charge of the investigation in the Justice Department and knew the latest developments, Nixon realized that he had to save his presidency—and himself. He decided his principle aides, Haldeman and Ehrlichman, had to go. After Gray was forced to resign his position as acting director of the FBI on April 27, the Watergate scandal erupted with the force of a volcanic explosion on April 30. It was astonishingly dramatic when President Nixon announced to the public on television that he had received the written resignations of Kleindienst, Haldeman and Ehrlichman, and had asked for and received the resignation of John Dean. Nixon made history in this way. Never, before this moment in American history, had people witnessed such a devastating toll of a President's top staff caused by scandal.

The result for the President himself was devastating, too. A clear sign of lack of power was imprinted on the presidency. The President's April 30 speech only fueled charges of wider scandal and stimulated pressures for a wider investigation. No matter how high the institutional position, as long as a person lost power in the collective power dynamics in the high political circle, his public standing would be deteriorating rapidly. Nixon experienced the same. In early April, a Gallup poll showed that the President had a nearly two-to-one approval rating, standing at 59 percent of respondents approving of his performance, 33 percent disapproving. The surveys for May 1–3 demonstrated a striking change, recorded at 48–40 percent approval/disapproval, with 12 percent now undecided. Ten days later, Gallup discovered the truly dramatic shift: 44 percent of respondents now approved of the President, while 45 percent disapproved.[39]

Nixon knew this better than anybody else. A few days before April 30th, he told Ron Ziegler, his Press Secretary: "It's all over, do you know that?" Nixon later realized that the day left him "so anguished and saddened that from that day on the presidency lost all joy for me." He noted that he had written his last full diary entry on April 14. "Events became so cheerless that I no longer had the time or the desire to dictate daily reflections."[40]

Historian Kutler remarked:

> The bright prospects for the second term had evaporated. The high expectations for fresh ideas and personnel were strangled at the outset, virtually stillborn as the President and his closest aides grappled with the growing tentacles of Watergate. Their struggles were futile; in effect, by April 30 the presidency of Richard Nixon was over. . . . Richard Nixon stood alone, naked to his enemies.[41]

More verifiable proof demonstrated the "on-death-bed" status of the Nixon presidency. Authority follows power; power establishes authority. If a person has power, he would be powerful everywhere. If he lost power, his institutional authority would be lost immediately. As Nixon's power dramatically declined, he was unable to display the normal presidential authority any more. Before April 1973, Congress' formal authority to distribute appropriations was reduced dramatically by the power of Presidents. Congress had failed in every effort to cut off funds to reduce the American involvement in the Vietnam War. The fact was clear—its formal institutional authority was not backed by the Washington collective power. But this time around, Nixon had to give in on the issue of Cambodian bombing despite the fact that traditionally and institutionally foreign policy was Presidents' turf. This would be a clear sign of Nixon's declining power.

Nixon's declining power also made him unable to firmly conduct his domestic policy. He had been unable to resist expensive increases in farm subsidies, Social Security benefits, and minimum wages. More seriously, his institutional authority was no longer effective enough to appoint his own troops. For the purpose of dealing with the Watergate investigation, Nixon had to embrace more diversified people in his administration under the pressure from the Washington collective power. He was forced to rely on peripheral forces as his core force was destroyed. One of the signs that made this apparent: the Massachusetts "liberal" Elliot Richardson replaced Arizona conservative Richard Kleindienst. Nixon also had no choice but to allow Archibald Cox to establish a "Kennedyite" beachhead in the government.[42]

This was the most important indication showing that Nixon stood at the brink of losing control of his own fate. His appointment of Elliot Richardson as Attorney General, the vital post as an arm of government to investigate the Watergate affair, to replace loyal Kleindienst, clearly indicated that Nixon had lost his interpersonal control of his troops and desperately needed a man with high credibility in Washington to restore his position in the Washington collective power. But at the same time, he gambled his fate in the hands of Richardson. Richardson was a moderate Republican from Massachusetts. In daily politics, he, together with New York governor Rockefeller, represented Nixon's rival faction in the Republican Party. Nixon could not control him because of his independent power base both within the party and in the public. Nixon, therefore, no longer had a protégé in such a vital post. This change dramatically shifted the climate in the Justice Department.

By mid-May, the prosecutors had effectively sealed their case against these President's men and officially pointed out the involvement of the President himself. When the U.S. Attorneys surrendered this case to Special Prosecutor Archbald Cox, they prepared a detailed eighty-seven-page summary of their efforts. The basic nature of the misdeeds and criminal violations by White House aides, CREEP staff, CIA and FBI leaders, and Justice Department officials were all clear by then. Most of the evidence came from the testimony of Dean, Magruder, various CREEP workers, and the Plumbers' chief operatives, Krogh and Young. For indicting these people, the charges were clear; for gaining convictions, there was some assembling work to do. That was the only thing left, according to Silbert. But, the major thing left was the role of the President.

At the end of his report, Silbert listed twenty-seven witnesses yet to be interviewed or presented to the grand jury. Richard Nixon was the number twenty-seven. Based on the President's post-break-in conversations with Haldeman, Ehrlichman, Helms, Walters—and most importantly, with Dean, Silbert wrote, "Were he not President, there is no question but that President Nixon would have to be questioned about a number of matters." Nixon's criminal culpability was no longer a suspicion, it was becoming a fact.[43]

In late May, Bernstein talked about the President's responsibility in the Watergate case on the phone with a Justice Department attorney. When he asked why they had not brought allegations against Nixon, the lawyer angrily rejected this assertion. He implied that they had gathered the necessary evidence, but evidence had nothing to do with the case. Assuming they had a case that showed the President was guilty of obstruction of justice, the problem was the Constitution. It was not clear at all how to deal with a president in a situation like this in the Constitution. The Constitution precluded the indictment of an incumbent President. If the President could not be indicted, the lawyers reasoned, he could not be called before a grand jury. A lawyer told Woodward: "The Watergate investigation has run smack into the Constitution." The inference became clear: it was not the matter of evidence. It was the unclear legal procedures that were blocking the way. Only the Supreme Court could untangle the issue.[44]

A critical move by Richardson, the new Attorney General, was to choose a Special Prosecutor, as he promised in his confirmation hearings to the senators on the Senator Judiciary Committee. After approaching somebody else, he finally chose his Harvard Law School Professor Archibald Cox. Cox was the least acceptable choice for Nixon because he represented the least likeable social groups: Harvard Law School professor, Massachusetts liberal, and a Kennedy loyalist. He had voted for McGovern and had close tie with the Kennedys. When he was sworn in as special prosecutor on May 24, Senator Edward Kennedy and Mrs. Robert Kennedy attended to show their support. It seemed that Richardson planted a time-bomb which would eventually destroy the Nixon presidency. Nixon wrote, "Unfortunately," as he put it, he had to give Richardson "absolute authority" to select a prosecutor, and thus "put the survival of my administration in his hands," and Richardson in turn had given it to a "partisan viper."[45]

Within days after he assumed office, Cox's appointments to positions in the Special Prosecutor's office raised further distress signals for Nixon. Cox first selected a Press Secretary, James Doyle, a prominent Washington newsman well known for his anti-Nixon views. He then chose two Harvard Law School colleagues for leading positions on his staff, following them with the staff appointment of James F. Neal, a forty-three-year-old Nashville attorney who had been the U.S. Attorney in that area and Robert F. Kennedy's special assistant from 1961 to 1964. Seven of the Special Prosecutor's eight-person senior staff had held office in the Kennedy and Johnson administrations. More than half the lawyers who served in the Special Prosecutor's office had graduated from the Harvard Law School.[46] It was no doubt that this group of people was motivated by a public spirit. But the mental frame of public spirit in their collective mind was their pursuit of the alleged wrongdoers with zeal, passion and a sense of absoluteness. In this way, this group of people would become the spearhead of the Washington collective power dynamics.

As the most powerful man in an institutional sense, Nixon was no longer in control of his own fate. The collective power dynamics had put his presidency on its death bed.

THE PATTERNED (BUT UNORGANIZED) COLLECTIVE PROCESS OF POWER

After Nixon's April 30th purge, Barry Goldwater continued to play a two-face role. He, on the one hand, praised the president's handling of the situation, defending Nixon on the Senate floor. On the other hand, Goldwater joined other senators in cosponsoring a resolution pressing Nixon to appoint a special prosecutor. Soon after, Goldwater, together with Senator Alan Cranston of California, even asked that the special prosecutor's charge be broadened to cover allegations of corruption beyond the Watergate break-in. Goldwater, on the one hand, rejected demands for Nixon's impeachment. However, on the other, he made it clear that if the president had "been dishonest about this, then I think impeachment would certainly come."[47]

On May 16, the day before the televised hearings of the Ervin Committee were to begin, Goldwater distributed a press release in which he warned "the loss of confidence in America's ability to govern." As proof, he cited the president's failure to fill a growing number of vacant positions in the Department of Defense. Discouraging economic news also put the nation at risk.[48]

Soon after, Goldwater wrote a private letter to Nixon, in which he expressed his strong emotional connection to Nixon as a long time ally: "I want you to understand that what I am saying to you comes right from the heart, comes from years of friendship and comes from deep devotion to everything you and I believe in." Goldwater then offered the President the means to reassert influence. It was important "to get acquainted with the Congress . . . getting down to the little fellow who has to go out and in his district or his state to keep the Republican Party going, to keep the radicals out of office and to support you." He suggested that the president "stop living alone. You have to tear down that wall that you have built around you. . . . No one who I know feels close to you. I will make one possible exception. I feel close to you." "I will continue to support you," he concluded, "back you, and as I have often told you, do anything you want me to."[49]

The next thing he did was rather dramatic and had much more significance in the entire Watergate saga. He gave John Dean a much-needed encouragement before the latter set out to publicly accuse Nixon of involvement in the cover-up. Goldwater and Dean had contact before their May 23 meeting at least once in April. Goldwater reported a conversation with John Dean, who had been Barry Jr.'s roommate at Saunton Military Academy. In that meeting Dean assured Goldwater that the allegation accusing Nixon's role in the cover-up was not true at all. Goldwater said he believed Dean.[50]

John Dean was scheduled to testify before the Ervin Committee on June 25, 1973, and commentators expected him to give evidence damaging to the President's case. In anticipation of his appearance, Dean solicited the advice of Goldwater. On May 23rd, a private meeting between Dean and Goldwater occurred in Goldwater's son, Congressman Barry Goldwater, Jr.'s apartment. The meeting before Dean's forthcoming testimony before the Senate Watergate Committee itself would mean something. "He told my dad what was going on," remembers the younger Goldwater. "He wanted to know whether he should be guarded or wide open in his testimony."[51]

Goldwater, as an important symbol of the conservative force in the nation that was a vital element of Nixon's support, was important to Dean. Dean wanted to evaluate the strength of the collective power that stood against Nixon. Personally, it was clear that liberals would be happy if he exposed the seamy side of the Nixon White House, but Dean knew that his roots of power, or of living, were not in the liberal camp. What he needed to know was how the conservative force would react to his testimony. His roots were in that camp. Politically, if Barry Goldwater advised him to take on Richard Nixon, it would be a clear sign that conservative forces were already alienated from Nixon. If that were the case, it would clearly mean that in the upcoming political trial of Watergate, Nixon would be effectively isolated. The battle would not simply be between the president and the congressional liberals but between Nixon and most powerful politicians. In that scenario, the fate of the Nixon presidency would be clear—the death of the Nixon presidency would be only a matter of time. Dean, therefore, would not need to be afraid of a man on his deathbed.

If Goldwater answered negatively the questions Dean asked, he would definitely make Dean have second thoughts about what he was going to say. But, during the meeting, when Dean asked the questions about national security, Goldwater replied firmly, no, he didn't know what verbal bombshells Dean might drop, but it was unlikely that real bombs would explode because of it. Then Dean started to ask the vital question about the internal power dynamics: What would happen if he weakened Nixon by testifying that he was lying about complete lack of involvement in the Watergate cover-up?

It was clear that Dean was about to charge the President of the United States publicly with offenses that might ruin him. Goldwater appeared calm. He said he did not see Dean's testimony would weaken the presidency—he did not see that problem; it didn't surprise him at all that Nixon lied. Nixon had been lying all his life. Goldwater's words were rather encouraging: "John, you just march your ass up there to the Senate, and in front of those cameras, and tell'em what you know as best you can. Sure a lot of sanctimonious people are going to say they're shocked to hear about their President doing these things. But don't think it's going to surprise anyone, really. Don't you worry about the consequences." Here, clearly, Goldwater had already separated Nixon from himself and the political forces he represented. Dean received much needed assurance.[52]

In an interview with Dan Rather of CBS in June after his meeting with Dean, Goldwater frankly expressed his real concern and his priority: "The thing that bothers me is here I have spent a third of my life trying to build the Republican Party, adding my little bit to it, having been successful in the South and in the Southwest, and then all of a sudden, as I near the end of my time in politics, I wonder—what the hell's it all been for?" [53]Clearly, Goldwater was ready to abandon Nixon for a larger cause—the power of the Republican Party and the power of himself in the Washington collective power dynamics, for which he had devoted almost all his political life.

By mid-May, Dean agreed to testify against the president of the United States. In the mean time, talking about impeachment was no longer viewed as black humor. The powerful politicians were fully involved by the collective power dynamics. Besides the Senate Select Committee, five other Congressional Committees joined to scrutinize the Nixon Administration's behavior. Their expedition took place in areas as wide as the sale of wheat to the Soviet Union, the settlement of an antitrust suit against ITT, and the domestic activities of the CIA. Equally significantly, a New York jury handed down indictments against John Mitchell and Maurice Stans for alleged campaign-law violations on May 10.[54]

However, the collective power dynamics bore their results slowly. Their unorganized nature would make the process zigzag for a long time. The Nixon presidency was on its deathbed but still breathing. The Senate Democratic Whip, Robert C. Byrd of West Virginia, was calling the idea of impeaching Nixon "at best premature and at worst reckless." On June 3, when Representative Paul McCloskey Jr. of California, who in 1972 had campaigned against Nixon for the Republican nomination, invited his fellow Republicans in the House to join in a discussion of Presidential impeachment, he was prevented by parliamentary maneuvering from this public airing of the subject. By June 12, several Congressmen were only able to gain the floor for a ninety-minute discussion of whether there were grounds for impeachment.[55] A *Christian Science Monitor* poll of nearly two hundred congressmen in mid-August 1973 showed an overwhelming number of them opposed forcing Nixon out by either impeachment or resignation.[56]

There were two forces that drove the power struggle in the Watergate investigation. First was the partisan one. The Democrats saw this as a great opportunity to inflict damage to the Republicans in order for themselves to get more money in fundraisers, more social connections in their networking activities, and more political influence in policy and legislative constructions, more votes in the elections, and more power. Republicans' concern was not that Nixon did anything morally or legally wrong but how to guard themselves in the rising tide of collective power against Nixon. They wanted to minimize the possibility of others in the Republican Party suffering after Nixon.

The second force was the one concerning the damage to the over-all power of all powerful political leaders in Washington, Democrats and Republicans alike. Ultimately, the capacity of dominance was the commonly shared power for all powerful political leaders in both parties, although they often engaged in blind fighting regardless of how harmful it would be to their common interest. But in the end after the new balance of power within themselves was reached, they would have to vindicate the capacity in order to continue their dominance. The collective power dynamics here revealed its unorganized but patterned nature. Most politicians in the high circle had sensed these two forces and had been struggling between them. On the surface, they were reacting to the immediate pressure of the collective power dynamics without paying much attention to the long term effect of their action. But in fact, the Washington collective power dynamics would provide a collective unconsciousness to all the political leaders. The long-term trajectory of their actions would follow this patterned collective unconsciousness.

Anyway, the Washington collective power was powerful enough to shift the political sentiment in the public domain. Only after those political leaders had dared utter the unutterable in the halls of Congress, did the notions of "resignation" and "impeachment" enter the public dialogue. It happened only months after Nixon's overwhelming public mandate. Another wave of fatal blows to the Nixon presidency was about to unfold in the public domain. The highly anticipated Ervin Committee's hearings were about to be put on the stage.

NOTES

1. Kutler, Stanley I. *The Wars of Watergate: The Last Crisis of Richard Nixon.* (New York: Knopf, 1990), 253.
2. Sirica, John J. *To Set the Record Straight: The Break-in, the Tapes, the Conspirators, the Pardon.* (New York: Norton, 1979), 91.
3. Sirica, *To Set the Record Straight,* 91
4. Dash, *Chief Counsel: Inside the Ervin Committee.* (New York: Random House, 1976), 26.
5. Dash, *Chief Counsel,* 27.
6. Kutler, *The Wars of Watergate,* 254.
7. Kutler, *The Wars of Watergate,* 255.
8. Dash, *Chief Counsel,* 33.
9. Dash, *Chief Counsel,* 27.
10. Sirica, *To Set the Record Straight,* 122.
11. Sirica, *To Set the Record Straight,* 120.
12. Dash, *Chief Counsel,* 34–35.
13. Dash, *Chief Counsel,* 45–51.
14. Dash, *Chief Counsel,* 56.
15. Dash, *Chief Counsel,* 57.
16. Spear, Joseph. *President and the Press: The Nixon Legacy.* (Cambridge, MA: Harvard University Press, 1984), 194.
17. Spear, *President and the Press,* 194.

18. Bernstein, Carl and Bob Woodward. *All the President's Men.* (New York: Simon & Schuster, 1974), 279–280.
19. Dash, *Chief Counsel*, 58.
20. Kutler, *The Wars of Watergate,* 290.
21. Kutler, *The Wars of Watergate,* 338; Bernstein and Woodward. *All the President's Men,* 322.
22. Thompson, Fred D. *At That Point in Time: The Inside Story of the Senate Watergate Committee.* (New York: Quadrangle, 1975), 38.
23. McQuaid, Kim. *The Anxious Years—America in the Vietnam-Watergate era.* (New York: Basic Books, 1989), 216
24. Kutler, *The Wars of Watergate,* 336.
25. Dean, John W. III. *Blind Ambition: The White House Years.* (New York: Simon & Shuster, 1976), 292–293.
26. Dash, *Chief Counsel*, 152.
27. Dean, *Blind Ambition,* 292–293.
28. Dash, *Chief Counsel*, 97; Kutler, *The Wars of Watergate,* 344.
29. Dash, *Chief Counsel*, 97.
30. Dash, *Chief Counsel*, 97.
31. Dash, *Chief Counsel*, 97–98.
32. McQuaid, *The Anxious Years,* 219.
33. McQuaid, *The Anxious Years,* 222.
34. McQuaid, *The Anxious Years,* 270.
35. Kutler, *The Wars of Watergate,* 270.
36. Goldberg, Robert Alan. *Barry Goldwater.* (New Haven, CT.: Yale University Press, 1995), 273.
37. Goldwater, Barry M. *With No Apologies—the personal and political memoirs of United States Senator Barry M. Goldwater.* (New York: William Morrow, 1979), 251.
38. Goldwater, *With No Apologies,* 251.
39. Kutler, *The Wars of Watergate,* 323.
40. Nixon, Richard M. *RN: The Memoirs of Richard Nixon* Vol.2. (New York: Grosset and Dunlap, 1978), 384.
41. Kutler, *The Wars of Watergate,* 320.
42. National Review, Aug. 17, 1973; Ehrlichman, John. *Witness to Power: The Nixon Years.* (New York: Simon & Schuster, 1982), 304–393.
43. Kutler, *The Wars of Watergate,* 337.
44. Bernstein and Woodward. *All the President's Men,* 322–323
45. Kutler, *The Wars of Watergate,* 332.
46. Kutler, *The Wars of Watergate,* 332–333.
47. Goldberg, *Barry Goldwater,* 275.
48. Goldberg, *Barry Goldwater,* 275.
49. Goldberg, *Barry Goldwater,* 276.
50. Goldwater, *With No Apologies,* 251.
51. Goldberg, *Barry Goldwater,* 276.

52. Dean, *Blind Ambition*, 295–297.
53. Kutler, *The Wars of Watergate*, 349.
54. Lang, Gladys Engel and Kurt Lang. *The Battle for Public Opinion—the President, the press, and the polls during Watergate.* (New York: Columbia University Press, 1983), 92.
55. Kutler, *The Wars of Watergate*, 380–381.

Chapter Four

The Difficulty of Genuine Communication in a Mass Society

REACHING-OUT:
CONNECTING WASHINGTON TO THE NATION

After the "April 30th explosion," it appeared that the Senate Committee had nothing more to do. On May 1st, Dash's staff gathered in his office with glum expressions on their faces. " 'Shit, it's almost all over before we have put on our first witness!' Terry Lenzner expressed the general feeling of the staff."[1]

But Dash knew better. He told his staff that their task was to prove the case to the public." He insisted that "It's our job to set the record straight—to put on the witnesses in public hearings to tell the Watergate story, not in the form of rumors or quotes from anonymous sources, but as participants and eyewitnesses to the facts."[2] Their task was clear: to push the victory beyond the high circle in Washington to the citizenry in general in order to consolidate it in a public forum.

For Ervin, the ultimate purpose of the Senate investigation would be "to inform Congress and the American people what high officials entrusted by the President with enormous governmental and political power had done."[3]

In a letter to Archbald Cox, who strongly opposed the public, televised Watergate hearings for fear of jeopardizing his criminal investigation and leading to all those guilty of Watergate offenses going free, Ervin wrote: "I'm frank to say that with the state of crisis in the country today due to the public's loss of confidence in its government—I believe it is more vital that the public be informed of the facts right now than that some people go to jail."[4] Dash remembered that what Ervin was worried about was the loss of confidence in government by the people. He sensed such a loss of confidence had reached such a critical stage that a national calamity was imminent. Therefore, some highly visible and responsible action by a branch of government must be taken.

In a mass society where citizens direct participation in the political process was very limited, the task here was to convince the citizens in general that the current system represented them without their direct participation. This was not an easy task. By its nature, the collective power dynamics were limited in the Washington beltway. The effectiveness of their connection to the nation was reflected and, at the same time, restrained by the nature of a mass society.

Generally speaking, the communication between those in power and the powerless was characterized by "symbolic imposition." It was a cultural arbitrary by an arbitrary power, as Pierre Bourdieu and Jean-Claude Passeron pointed out.[5] The purpose was the affirmation of the political leaders' values and the infallibility of these leaders. It would be clear that this was an asymmetrical power relationship. As a consequence, the most serious problem would be the absence of a genuine interest on the part of the citizens in what was being communicated. For the purpose of stimulating a genuine concern for the effectiveness of communication and making sure it was shared by all the participants, it was essential to minimize the antagonistic leader-led relationship. Genuine communication must be based on genuine interest. The Washington political leaders, to some degree, successfully achieved this goal and therefore framed and shaped the minds and hearts of ordinary citizens.

Like most political struggles within the camp of the political leaders only, Watergate was a story that ordinary people would have hard time understanding. Powerful politicians must mobilize the symbolic system effectively in order to clarify and communicate the gravity and meaning of this struggle. The more severe the struggle was, the harder, deeper, and broader the symbolic framing should be. That is to say, they had to tell the public, like most parents educate their children, why this thing was important, why they should engage in this thing so seriously. They must communicate on the high road with a heavy moral tone and social justification. This was the true meaning of public education. Otherwise, with cynicism prevailing, most ordinary people would be confused about the nature of the Watergate charges, or even have difficulty believing Watergate as a problem worthy of their attention.

How did those political leaders use the symbolic system in order to frame the nature of Watergate? The ways they did this would be by manipulating the procedure of the exposing process, by the way they highlighted some events, by the context within which they framed these events, by the language they used to frame the developments of those events, and, especially, by linking news and selectively publicized fact to symbols familiar to the ordinary citizens.

Concretely speaking, merely winning the public's attention was far from enough; the usual way of broadcasting would not be acceptable. It was too commercialized; it was designed to dramatize the event in order to get attention. The press still treated the ordinary people, to some degree, as active agents with distinctive subjective desire and needs, although these desire and needs were broken into pieces and then channeled, reduced or promoted. But, in the case of Watergate coverage, it would be necessary to reshape ordinary people's very desires and needs. Therefore, the key was public education. As Dash asserted: the public hearings "had to create public understanding of the Watergate facts and produce a significant public response."[6]

As the majority counsel, Dash was in charge of implementing this whole idea of symbolic construction. First, it was essential for the hearings to be broadcast live on TV.

At the time when Haldeman, Ehrlichman, and Colson were still in power and Nixon's power had not diminished so dramatically, the ability of the White House to be a formidable foe was still there. The TV networks still had lingering fear of the Nixon administration. Also, they didn't want to lose advertising revenue. They considered live TV coverage as too costly both politically and financially. The "April 30th explosion" exposed Nixon's weakness in the power struggle to the public. Few people would fear a person on his deathbed. On the contrary, it would be tempting to join the parade and share some credit. TV networks started to change their attitude.

Dash planned to call for a long witness list and a rejection of a "bombshell" opening. Instead, the hearings would start out with little-known witnesses in order to provide the details necessary for the public to understand the background roles and activities of the major witnesses. However, most politicians were only agents of their own immediate selfish interests. Those interests were not necessarily in accordance with the government system on which all of them were relying. Many times they were blinded to the macro-structural picture. People are hardly purely rational in terms of making the most from the system in a long run. Only the clear signals of the collective power dynamics would be able to move them.

Two Democratic Senators, Talmadge and Inouye, could not see Ervin and Dash's idea through. They were going to run for re-election in 1974. Their sense was that their voters would not be happy if the hearings prolonged as long as Dash planned. Their strategy was still the one used in the normal years. They only tried to channel and promote certain needs and wants of their voters in a retail fashion. They did not recognize that in this unusual year, they had a need to change their strategy to reshape their voters' minds and hearts on a wholesale scale. As the major players on the offensive side of a power struggle, they must rationalize and justify their actions in the Watergate struggle and, more importantly, convince their voters the system that bestowed them power also worked for their voters. They must make sense of the struggle by framing it as good and necessary. They must frame their power struggle as a benevolent action for the benefit of society as a whole. Only if they could do so successfully, could their victory be consolidated and their purpose of public education be achieved. Because they did not see this important aspect of a power struggle deep enough and far enough, the two Democratic Senators on the Ervin Committee thought their re-election campaign would be damaged by a lengthy hearing. They were reluctant to support Ervin and Dash at this time as they usually did.

On the Republican side, because they were not on the offensive side, they did not need to justify the offensive action in order to look good in the eyes of their voters. They did not see the system upon which their dominance relied, either. At this point, a mere bi-partisan appearance would be good enough and such an appearance did not in any way prevent the power struggle behind the scenes. It was clear that, under the overwhelming offensive pressure from the other side of the struggle, Baker and other Republicans he represented knew it was impossible to stop the offensive. Therefore, what they needed to do was to restrict the other side's offensive for the benefit of their position in this Watergate power struggle. On the table, they would openly try to use "balance and fairness" to slow down the investigation. Behind the scenes, they tried very hard to end the investigation as quickly as possible in order to minimize the damage done to those in their own ranks. Senator Baker's plan demonstrated a part of Republican's strategy. He planned a brief set of hearings—a few days of witnesses on Watergate, followed up by a few days of witnesses on dirty tricks and then a few days of witnesses on campaign financing. The entire public hearings should be finished at the end of June or early July. The Committee report would be written over the summer.[7]

The blind power struggle and the need for connecting the Washington Beltway to the entire nation became conflicting. Ervin was very much against Baker's plan. He was firm; he was skillful. His interpersonal maneuvering in the process highlighted the importance of interpersonal power dynamics in the political process. In the end, Ervin prevailed. Formal institutions depended on this type of informal dynamics rather than vice versa. The struggle inside the Ervin Committee on this crucial issue was significant for us to understand the way of connection between Washington and the nation.

After the failure on the substantive issue, Baker struggled for a procedural one. He recommended that senators on the Committee question the witnesses while the staff only play a supportive role. It was clear that he did not want to submit all the control of the hearings to the aggressive majority staff who were carrying out Ervin's strategy. But technically, the staff were the only people who were thoroughly prepared on the testimony; they were the only people who were familiar with all the relevant piece of evidence and would be able to challenge testimonies of witnesses. Only they could make sure that all the essential facts were presented in an orderly manner. It was only because of Ervin's strong support that Baker's idea was rejected by the Senators on the Committee.[8]

It was clear that the force that drove the hearing planning process was not the institution-oriented individual rationality; rather, it was Ervin and his skillful use of interpersonal and collective power dynamics that made a difference. It was also clear that the way of connection between Washington and the nation was also decided by such a collective power dynamic.

THE ERVIN COMMITTEE HEARINGS

Such a micro-interpersonal dynamics moved the macro-structural process. Beginning on May 17, 1973, the hearings of the Ervin Committee were televised gavel-to-gavel. There would be 37 days of hearings, not ending until August 7 after 237 hours of coverage. The cross-examination took place before the cameras. Ordinary citizens could watch the exchanges between the seven-man committee and the 33 former members of the White House staff or employees of the Nixon reelection committee. They could watch as much as they cared to. During the daytime, one station broadcast the hearings. At night, some 150 to 160 public television stations carried a full replay of the day's hearings. The evening news and the next morning's headlines would pick up whatever was revealed during the hearings. Those unable to watch TV could listen to the radio or catch the highlights in newspapers. Few people, however uninterested or bent on avoiding the hearings, could extricate themselves from entering people's everyday conversations about what they saw and heard about Watergate. The pervasive power of the mass media fully presented itself.[9] However, how much people could be changed was another story.

The problem of genuine communication via mass media was first revealed by the fact that mass media as a whole was a commercial entity after all. Because of this fact, the start of the media coverage of the hearings was a little rough. A week before the hearings began on May 17, public television committed itself to live coverage, but the executives of the three commercial networks still hesitated because of financial concerns. Having decided to cover the first day's proceedings at the last minute, the networks chose to remain flexible thereafter. A CBS official expressed the typical fear: "200,000 nice little old ladies whose favorite soap opera had been pre-empted by something called Watergate would call in and complain." By the second day of the hearings, the networks complained that the hearings had attracted only 9.5 million viewers, down more than 4 million from their normal audiences. By the end of the first week, ABC and CBS revealed that their callers were speaking ten to one against live coverage. Most were angry: "We're sick of nothing but Watergate, Watergate." "Watergate is being shoved down our throats" "You're hurting the President." Therefore, by the beginning of the second week, the networks reached an unprecedented agreement among themselves to rotate live coverage, in order to satisfy "viewer discontent." Another discontent was in the boardrooms—each hour of pre-empted programming lost the networks an estimated $120,000 in advertising revenues.[10]

The second obstacle to genuine communication that had to be overcome was the issue of stimulating genuine interest among citizens. Generally speaking, regular viewers of the proceedings were better educated and of higher socioeconomic status than nonviewers. But there was a considerable overlap of these characteristics between viewers and nonviewers. An interesting point here was that, as a study in Florida showed, nonviewers were almost as likely as viewers to believe Nixon was guilty of something. They believed Nixon had prior knowledge of both the break-in and the subsequent cover-up. They just did not want to hear about it.

The reason for this phenomenon was that nonviewing, in many cases, reflected a deep-rooted distrust of politics and politicians. The Langs concluded: "distrust . . . to have been especially typical of nonviewers who identified with no political party but had voted for Nixon in 1972."[11]

As the coverage went on, however, Americans watched the Watergate proceedings in steadily growing numbers, rather evenly spread across sections, age groups, and educational backgrounds. The overall viewer size and sustained interest exceeded all expectations. Compared to most public affairs broadcasts, these hearings achieved extraordinarily high ratings. According to Nielsen statistics, the best estimate of total exposure was some 30 hours per television home. By early August, according to a national Gallup survey, nearly 90 percent of all Americans had watched some part of the hearings.[12]

The hearings did change the mind of one group of viewers: those who had voted for Nixon in 1972 and were paying "a great deal of attention" to the hearings. At the conclusion of Dean's testimony in late June, 46 percent of Gallup's respondents said they would still vote for Nixon against McGovern, down some 16 percent since the November election. But following testimony by Nixon's chief aides, the polls for the first time showed that a majority of citizens regarded Watergate as a "serious matter." Nixon's rating in the Harris poll had fallen from 57 percent positive before the hearings to 32 percent afterward. The Gallup poll showed a similar result. Nixon's rating was down

9 points in four weeks and 37 point since January. "Replays" of the 1972 election suggested that Nixon might not have won had the hearings been conducted before the time of the election in the previous Fall.[13]

It was clear that faith in Nixon had been shaken by the public hearings. Citizens in general in increasing numbers simply did not believe in Nixon. A Gallup telephone poll showed that 77 percent of the nation heard his televised defense on August 15, but only a little over one-fourth of the audience believed him. Forty-four percent considered him "not at all convincing."[14]

It is worth noting that all of these results were achieved via television. As many critics might say, this is typically the case in mass society. The communication via TV had the nature of a one-way street. It was imposed on the viewers by the people who conducted the show. It was hard to develop any deep rooted genuine communication via TV, especially a relationship of an interpersonal and collective nature between the people inside the Washington beltway and the people around the nation. To those outside the Washington power circles, the hearings were like a soap opera come to life. There was a dramatic contrast between the scene inside the Washington beltway and the scene outside of it. Inside, what worked were the interpersonal and collective power dynamics that touched deeply on each power player. However, the means to expand the inside collective power dynamics to the outside of the Washington beltway was so limited and so superficial. The connection between Washington and the nation was therefore weak. No matter how hot the scenario was inside Washington, people around the nation could only be connected to it by a cold, motionless TV.

Because of this weak and superficial connection, the educational effect of the Ervin Committee hearing did not go along with what Ervin and many others originally expected. It did not redeem the credibility of the political system. Still, many citizens remained skeptical about the government. The political leaders in Washington wished to prove something about Richard Nixon but did not want to hurt the government in general. They wanted to prove that "no one is above the law" and the laws upon which the nation was dependent were just and effective. However, when it came to the mind of ordinary citizens, eloquence often evaporated into knee-jerk phrases: "Nixon is a crook"; "Nixon got railroaded"; and, most harmful, "All politicians are only out for themselves." What Watergate reflected was not a rationalized and institutionalized government in textbooks. It was a struggle for power inside high political circles. Some were destroyed; some gained more power and rose to higher positions. As a commentator put it:

> Watergate produced a result which Vietnam never had. The war made the United States look ineffective and divided, but Watergate made America look ridiculous

in the eyes of its own people. The leaders often appeared to be buffoons, and the led hedged their political loyalties accordingly. The view that "government is the problem" grew. Washington looked as illegitimate and pathetic as it did misguided or criminal.[15]

As many citizens became more disillusioned and withdrawn, a conservative trend was strengthened. It regarded the government as a problem rather than a solution. This became a long-term trend and its effect had yet to be exhausted several decades later. At the same time, another unexpected result of the hearings was that it not only developed into an open window for citizens in general to see the invisible side of the government, it also pushed democracy beyond the normal five-minute spectacle.

Despite its limitation, the attempt of constructing genuine communication itself produced dramatic result. Witnesses marched across the television landscape, exposing matters that normally lay deeply hidden behind the allmighty political system. A fascinated viewing public gleaned lessons in political behavior not usually found in textbooks. The committee's conduct and the information yielded by the hearings stood in stark contrast to the image and information conveyed by the popular myth of the government. Citizens, especially those unorganized ones who had little opportunity to get a glance at the political process in high places, had to think about and even rethink some of their taken-for-granted assumptions about the political process.

For many citizens, the hearings were widely heralded as having provided a "unique civic lesson in American democracy." They felt they were treated as a jury and thus got a sense of participation. Such a sense rarely happened in their daily lives. The hearings increased a sense of public participation by both organized and unorganized citizens in government activities. It was the most important consequence of the full coverage of the hearings, which had allowed people to "see for themselves" and "to judge as juries." During and after the hearings, public awareness and understanding grew and their movement toward action emerged. Unorganized citizens might not quite understand the Constitutional doctrines about the First and Fourth Amendments, but the hearings made a large segment of them suddenly discover an instinct deeply embedded in their minds and hearts: that checks and balances of the system were not working to protect them; that they needed to participate in the political process for their own protection by their own action. The Washington politicians would suddenly discover that the roots of democracy might be deeper than they knew after they witnessed the citizen's reaction to the "Saturday Night Massacre."

The periods of quiet immediately following the hearings were deceptive. The sense of public awareness and public participation developed into an overwhelming negative response to the "Saturday Night Massacre." The so called "truly dramatic shift in opinion and pattern of citizen's action following the 'Saturday Night Massacre'" was nonetheless a continuing response to the hearings.[16] The outpouring of outrage two months later was a continuing response to what was observed and learned by viewing the hearings. The hearings thus set the framework for subsequent events.

THE WAY THINGS WERE

Nixon was on his deathbed politically. A legislative effort to embarrass and weaken Nixon had, suddenly and unexpectedly, turned into a struggle that destroyed him. But, what made the "Saturday Night Massacre" happen? It was clear that the incident caught almost everyone in the Washington political circle by surprise. It was unexpected that an almost dead Nixon still had the energy to put up a deathbed struggle. However, it was the conflicting action of those powerful politicians that led to this drama.

The Senate Committee's public hearings were right in the middle of the growing perception that Watergate was something larger than a break-in, larger even than a high-level cover-up. Those Washington politicians could handle the collective power dynamics inside Washington but did not have the means to connect themselves to the nation as a whole. The means for them to reach-out out of Washington was too superficial and limited. During and after the Senate Select Committee hearings, they started to realize the reality.

Washington insiders knew that there were so many complicated political crimes deeply rooted and deeply embedded in the existing political system. Almost all Washington insiders knew that most powerful politicians were vulnerable under investigation. As Woodward and Bernstein asserted, there were "rats' nests" all over Washington. If Watergate stimulated a certain investigatory atmosphere, it would have the potential to become pervasive, uncontrollable, and frivolous. If it were not brought under control, there would be many, many others, not just Nixon, swept up.[17] For instance, according to Woodward and Bernstein, Senator minority leader Hugh Scott himself was involved in a series of appointments to government jobs, which had bypassed Civil Service regulations. In fact, Scott was the worst offender on the Hill, particularly with regard to the General Service Administration. GSA chief Arthur Sampson was Scott's man. The two of them operated the GSA as if they were running a private employment agency. Firms okayed by Scott had been awarded GSA contracts in various irregular ways.[18]

What they needed to do was to narrow down the scope from Nixon = the current political system to Nixon = Watergate, and further narrowing down Watergate = all political crimes to Watergate = break-in + cover-up. The

Washington politicians thus tried to reframe the issue. The idea was that, with Nixon as the villain, the governance system would be vindicated and all others who did similar crimes would be saved; with the break-in and cover-up as the only crimes needing to be punished, all other crimes, like illegal campaign contributions and illegal patronages, would no longer be visible to the ordinary citizens. Overall, anything that might lead citizens to question the governance system as a whole and the whole group of powerful politicians as individuals would be covered by Nixon only for his behavior of breaking-in and covering-up. In this way, they could keep "the way things are in Washington." As Drew pointed out: " 'Washington' can become accustomed to the way things are. . . . 'Washington' knew that the campaign-contribution laws had been flouted since, it seemed, the beginning. . . . It knew these things. It just didn't talk about them much. That was the way things worked."[19]

For the purpose of getting rid of Nixon as an individual without hurting the Washington collective power as a whole, those political leaders chose to go two parallel routes: politically soft and legally aggressive.

It would be clear that, after the heated summer hearings, the political route was not safe. It might easily get out of control because it would be natural to expand such an investigation into other areas led by the countless and complicated connections among those powerful politicians. On the contrary, the legal way would be much more specific and could be narrowly defined and tightly controlled. The legal route was regarded as the best way to solve the Watergate affair within the system under effective control.

Furthermore, the "rule of law" would make the power struggle look like legitimate. Generally speaking, those Washington politicians must rely on a symbolic system to rule and dominate the vast population of more than two hundred million. The legal system was an essential part of this symbolic system that could successfully transform power into authority for the winners in a power struggle. But, this approach caused an unexpected consequence: on the one hand, they offered Nixon an iota of political energy for him to launch his deathbed adventure; on the other hand, their extreme legal pressure and lack of clear legal construction to solve the legal deadlock between Cox and Nixon pushed Nixon onto a risky road. Their action after the summer actually paved the way to a major incident like the "Saturday Night Massacre."

Nixon was hanging in there legally after the April 30 explosion. No smoking gun was found by the end of the public hearings. The constitutional impasse before the hearings was still there. The only progress in the legal sense was the discovery of the White House taping system. The Nixon tapes provided an opportunity to return the case from the public arena back into the hands of those legal professionals. The White House taping system was discovered accidentally during the hearings. But once it was exposed, it took on a life of its own. The Nixon tapes became the best evidence in a criminal proceeding and the court and the Special Prosecutor focused their attention on obtaining them. Nixon's refusal to produce those tapes subpoenaed by the Special Prosecutor pushed him on the legal death road after he was already on his death-bed politically.

It was interesting to consider what this story would be like if those tapes were not revealed. It was clear that Nixon was already politically on his deathbed before the taping system was exposed. The talk of impeachment and resignation had begun several months before people heard about the tapes. But those tapes were significant in a legal battle. How different, then, would the legal proceedings have been in a situation without those tapes?

It was clear that both the U.S. Attorney's office and the staff of the Senate Select Committee had already possessed documents in abundance regarding the involvement of Nixon and his top aides. If there were no tapes, there must be something else to fight for. They might be Nixon's daily news summary — according to Dean, almost all of Nixon's instructions were written on them; they might be some internal "eye-only" memos, or whatever.[20] The key was that for pushing the process forward, Nixon's opponents needed something to continue the battle on legal grounds. The hearings created a political situation in which those Washington politicians must finish the battle in the legal field. What they must do was to find a legal solution to narrow down the issue in order to end the case cleanly. The Nixon tapes provided the most convenient material object for this purpose. Once the typing system was accidentally found, the trajectory of the Watergate investigation was set onto a new irreversible direction. All the important incidents thereafter were tied closely to those tapes and those tapes became the fatal weapon to terminate Nixon's political life and the Watergate saga.

At the same time, those Washington politicians started softening their political pressure as the summer ended. The collective power dynamics in Washington changed their direction.

The Republicans on the Senate Select Committee played a role as cooler from day one in the hearings during the heated summer. On the surface, they tried to project an image of fairness. Underneath, their objective was to limit the proceedings within the realm of Watergate and focus on Nixon and his principal aides' actions around it. They used any opportunity to shorten the proceedings, as they originally attempted.

As early as July 28, 1973, Fred Thompson regarded "the committee's honeymoon with the nation was over." He appraised an article in Washington Star News and thus revealed his own thought at that point: "Ehrlichman, if he wasn't entitled to better treatment than the other witnesses, was nevertheless entitled to better than he got." Dash got more and more attacks, Thompson said, because he lost some of the precision, composure, and sense of fairness. The Ervin Committee had been attacked for being a little too full of itself, a little too eager to take on and to bring down Haldeman and Ehrlichman.[21]

The Committee members started showing uneasiness about the Committee's hearings. On the Republican side, once extremely zealous Senator Weicker dramatically changed his path. Rather than trying to go one-step ahead of those Democratic members on the Committee to uncover more of Nixon and his men's misdeeds, he started questioning the procedure and fairness of the hearings. At the same time, Baker's idea about shortening the hearings got more and more echoes from those Democratic members on the committee. At the session on July 23, Talmadge reiterated his belief that the nation was getting tired of Watergate. A week later he suggested that the committee "expedite" the hearings, even if it meant giving up the Senate's August recess. Even Ervin suggested some insignificant witnesses could be dropped in order to shorten the proceedings.[22]

Dash started feeling disappointment about the Senators on the Committee after Labor Day when those Senators came back from their August recess. He recorded: "When the Senate Watergate Committee reconvened after the long August recess, the members displayed little of the vim and vigor that had got them through the extraordinary pace and high drama of the Committee's public hearings during the spring and summer."[23] Although the Committee's heavy mail still demonstrated the heated public interest, their "back home" advisers advised them otherwise. Most of the Senators referred to the public as ever impatient. They claimed that the public had grown tired of the committee's public hearings and wanted an end to Watergate. Talmadge reminded the Committee that Congress would go on recess again on October 15 and urged that that date as a cutoff date for all further public hearings of the committee. Dash was especially disappointed that Ervin appeared amenable to Talmadge's suggestion.

The contents of the Committee investigation were also limited to break-in and cover-up. But as Dean described, the real purpose for the cover-up from its very beginning was about protecting the illegal contributions and those behind-the-scene contributors.[24]

It was very ironical that Dash correctly but at the same time naively insisted that the Watergate break-in and cover-up were only one part of the public hearings. He insisted that the Committee's public hearings on unethical and illegal political espionage and campaign financing during the presidential campaign of 1972 was more important for the political reform of the electoral process and the education of the American people.[25] It would be very clear that he did not recognize an important fact: if the hearings were expanded into a broad field, it would expose the whole seamy side of the governance system. It was only because of this that his aggressive strategy had become no longer tolerable to his bosses.

Elizabeth Drew observed and recorded the action taken by Congress after it reconvened. She said: "The Ervin Committee started showing signs of losing its nerve, and direction." When most of the returning politicians talked about the fact that "the country" was tired of Watergate, "It may be that it is the politicians who are tiring of Watergate, and want to get it behind them.[26]

Drew saw through these Senators' motivation behind their behavior. She pointed out that the politicians "sense that Watergate is lowering still further the public's esteem for politics." They had become uneasy about the fact that the Ervin Committee was going to conclude its hearings on the actual break-in at the Watergate and move toward the beginning of hearings on campaign practices and money. For Washington political leaders, they could easily say they did not break into their opposition's campaign headquarters. In this way, they could uncouple themselves from Nixon. But the exploration of campaign money would make them eliminate the difference between them and Nixon. Many of them "did flout the spirit, and some even the letter, of the laws covering the raising and spending of campaign funds."[27]

This was a clear sign about the shifting collective power dynamics. In Drew's words, this kind of move went through the "Washington nervous system." As Drew described, the Washington power dynamics drove the nervous system. Political players in Washington were "investors in power." Their careers and fortunes depended on "recognizing and spotting shifts in power."[28]

Here, news became event. The Washington collective power dynamics was reflected by this "nervous system". Some Washington insiders estimated that the President's position became stronger. A Nixon assistant told Drew that the worst was over for the President. He even talked about the President reestablishing his popularity—a foreign-policy crisis might good enough to divert attention from Watergate and reassert the President's capacity for leadership in the foreign-policy field.[29]

The news people in the press were certainly influenced by the news. Their profession made them very sensitive to the collective power dynamics in Washington. News more easily became event among those journalists who produced news. The event here at this time was that Watergate was no longer so attractive to those drama-seeking journalists because they sensed the fading interests among those powerful politicians. The networks ended live television coverage of the Senate hearings after October 3, 1973. The drama was over up to this point. The more fundamental Dash and his assistants were going to display to those powerful politicians, the less dramatic effect since they were the daily routine in Washington. Because these were done collectively by those powerful politicians and did not violate the codes that safeguard the collective interests of those powerful as a whole, nobody cared to change anything. The collective power dynamics inside Washington did not allow such change to happen. "The way things always are" was certainly not dramatic and less attractive. Daniel Schorr of CBS pointed it out to Dash sharply: "You've got to be politically naive to think that the stuff you're now dealing with is worth the bother." Schorr was not alone with this view. Several news reporters had even used the same charge against Dash in their stories. Dash had a hard time understanding them and still believed the issue was so fundamental and the public was interested in how the political campaigns were run.[30]

There was no dispute about the facts. The difference between Dash and his bosses was that those powerful politicians did not like the idea of letting citizens know too much about their activities. The connection between Washington and the nation was so weak and superficial that it could not sustain any further public shock. It was indeed naïve trying to pursue a full exposure of all the problems in the system and of the system.

"SATURDAY NIGHT MASSACRE"

At the same time, the legal pressure was still aggressively on without the support of the collective power dynamics inside Washington. The issue of whether the President should obey a court decision on the tapes had become the focus. Nixon was forced in a legal corner. He only had two choices, either of them would, no doubt, ruin him. The first choice for Nixon would be to hand over the tapes requested by Cox and, thus, expose his illegal activities; a second would be resisting Cox's request, which was in a form of court order issued by the trial court and upheld by the Appeals Court, and therefore facing legal consequences. Clearly, Nixon was in a no-win situation. All of these set the stage for a Nixon's deathbed attack.

Just at this moment, a foreign war—the Yom Kippur War in the Middle East—suddenly erupted. Nixon quickly seized this opportunity to make a big move. He first tried to force a compromise. He pursued Attorney General Richardson to convince Cox to accept the tape transcripts instead of original tapes. The transcripts were supposed to be verified by Senator Stennis. This was so called the "Stennis Compromise." It was clear that there was no legal base for such an arrangement. Cox refused this deal. Desperately, Nixon ordered Cox to be fired. Richardson and Associate Attorney General Ruckelshaus refused to carry out the order and resigned. The events of October 20 happened so surprisingly and swiftly. The removing of Archibald Cox and resignations of highest rank Justice Department officials happened all of a sudden. The images of FBI agents sealing the Special Prosecutor's office and barring access to Cox's staff shocked and frightened the nation. It was compared to the Reichstag fire that was the prelude to the rise of Hitler.[31]

At this point, the collective power dynamics inside Washington were forced to change by the nation. The result of the October 20 event was not only opposite to what Nixon and his lawyers had anticipated, but also surprised those Washington politicians. They had softened their political pressure and had been trying aggressively to solve the legal confrontation over the Nixon tapes between Archibald Cox and Nixon. Several Senators became involved in the "Stennis compromise". But Nixon made an unexpected move that stimulated national emotions.

It was surprising to see the citizens' reaction. Citizens were mobilized. It became a key fact in the power dynamics immediately after the incident. The event raised a "firestorm" of public protest. The public revulsion was extraordinarily massive and went far beyond the Washington collective power dynamics. It temporarily developed into a national collective power dynamics. As Theodore H. White described: "The reaction that evening was near instantaneous as it had been at Pearl Harbor, or the day of John F. Kennedy's assassination—an explosion as unpredictable and as sweeping as mass hysteria."[32]

The responses of Washington political figures and media commentators were predictable, but new voices were also heard. The turmoil spread. Deans of seventeen law schools (including Harvard, Columbia, Yale, Stanford) joined in a petition that Congress "consider the necessity" of impeachment now. At Columbia, one of the deans called the President "a paranoid egomaniac, a quintessentially hollow man."[33] Chesterfield Smith, the President of the American Bar Association, told his group that Nixon's actions had threatened the rule of law and the administration of justice.[34]

Many established social groups were mobilized. The AFL-CIO was the largest and most important organization to lead a drive to impeach Nixon. The AFL-CIO represented a hundred and eleven unions, with a total membership of nearly fourteen million workers. The Union passed a resolution denouncing Nixon. Its leader, George Meany, called on the President to resign. Meany said the labor federation would call for Nixon's impeachment if he refused to resign.[35] However, the real shock was the grassroots protest. It began within an hour of Ziegler's statement with the honking of cars outside the White House. Protesters gathered rapidly holding up signs saying, "HONK FOR IMPEACHMENT." The media worked more as a messenger than as an advocator or opinion leader. NBC and CBS arranged a ninety-minute special show, which spread consternation nationwide. However, telegraphic response began to spurt even before their shows were off the air. By Tuesday morning

Western Union had processed more than 150,000 telegrams ("the heaviest concentrated volume on record"); by Wednesday evening the volume had reached 220,000. At the end of ten days the total was 450,000. An important phenomenon should be noted here. One of the Congressmen insisted that the protest was "not organized" and was a "grassroots" phenomenon. (Human Event, November 3, 1973) One Congressman told Elizabeth Drew that the public protest against Nixon in his district was from "basic middle-of-the-road types who had voted for the President."[36]

However, in such a big public outcry, the core of the grassroots protests were church goers and students. The most denunciations and rallies were composed of people who were in some social organizations or in socially closely knitted settings, like colleges or universities where students lived and studied together and were closely connected. At Duke Law School, Nixon's alma mater, 350 students petitioned for the removal of Nixon's portrait from Duke's student courtroom.[37]

The Washington politicians clearly felt the heat of ordinary citizens' movement. It was "as if a dam had broken," said one Congressman. Republican Senator Javits of New York reported that of the 1,150 messages he received after the Cox dismissal, less than ten supported the President.[38] Shortly after the incident, Senator James Buckley and three of the most conservative Republicans in the House reported that their mail was running 90 percent in favor of impeachment. Many House Republicans and Southern Democrats who had supported Nixon felt the public pressure. Ray Thornton of Arizona and Tom Railsback of Illinois touched the "storm of mail".[39]

The national collective power dynamics forced those Washington politicians' hands. Up until that event most members of Congress were trying to put off doing anything, but this event forced them to do something. A telephone survey by David Broder of the *Washington Post* brought the responses from the leaders of Republican Party: the Wyoming Republican Chairman Jack Speight: "I just can't believe what's going on in that zoo. It's like 'tune in tomorrow for next adventure,'" Minnesota Republican National Committeeman Rudy Boschwitz: "You've heard of that play, Stop the World, I Want to Get Off. That's how I feel right now." Republican Governor of Michigan William Milliken: "I deplore what happened. It's a setback in efforts to restore public confidence in government. . . . Clearly we face a constitutional crisis."[40]

Elizabeth Drew talked with a Republican member of the House, a leader among the moderate Republicans after the event. He told Drew that "Everyone around here is terribly depressed—kind of worn down by the sequence of events. It's taken over everything. People have their heads down. They don't talk up anymore. They don't know what to say. It's a pretty unpleasant business."[41] He deeply sensed the damage done by the Watergate scandal and Watergate investigation. The Washington collective power dynamics were pushed by the national collective power dynamics—a situation that felt so uncomfortable. The strong grassroots reaction after the "Saturday Night Massacre" made many "old-timers" in the Congress, who were not accustomed to such a heavy load, think, as a Congressman described, that politics was becoming "more trouble than it's worth."[42] For this kind of Congressmen, the sooner the affair ended, the better.

A Democratic Senate aide who was in the traffic patterns of Capitol Hill told Drew about the deeper reason why people were depressed and wanted Nixon to go sooner than later. According to this person, "Nixon's 'days are numbered' because of issues that 'won't stay hidden'".[43] So many Nixon's misdeeds were exposed, which inevitably connected to the system as a whole. The situation had made everybody inside Washington look bad.

Nixon got everybody into trouble and made the Washington collective power dynamics unworkable. So they were angry; they were mad. Such a strong sense had stimulated a strong sentiment of getting rid of this "bad apple". They must act in order to pre-empt the power dynamics from outside Washington by reasserting the Washington collective power dynamics. But they had to proceed cautiously. For the purpose of regaining initiative and moving ahead in an orderly manner, House Speaker Carl Albert of Oklahoma quickly met with the Democratic leaders of the House on Monday, October 22nd, two days after the "Saturday Night Massacre." They evaluated the situation together and "then agreed that an inquiry must be set up immediately, to head off any stampede of floor resolutions which might, in the atmosphere of passion and street turbulence, cause impeachment to be voted instantly."[44]

Most of the Washington politicians therefore still insisted on finishing the case in orderly fashion through the legal route. Even the most active members of the liberal wing of the Democratic Party thought so. On November 5, a Democratic senator told Elizabeth Drew that he thought the talk of resignation was "politically premature." He told Drew: "If we are going to impeach him, we need more facts. That is why we must proceed with the Special Prosecutor."[45]

In this way, the "Saturday Night Massacre" pushed Congress back into an active role. The political pressure officially merged into the legal battle; the House of Representatives, a political body but with decisive legal power, became the major player from that point on. It worked with professional bodies in the government—the Special Prosecutor's Office with Jaworski as the new Special Prosecutor succeeding Cox, the D.C. court, and the Supreme Court—to finish the case up.

The House of Representatives' decisive legal power to finish the Watergate affair was its authority to impeach the President. The impeachment process was officially and openly set in motion on October 23. House Speaker Carl Albert stated that he would refer all impeachment resolutions to the Judiciary Committee. Within two days, 84 representatives, including one Republican, had introduced a total of 22 bills and resolutions calling for impeachment or, at the least, impeachment inquiry. Despite Nixon's yielding on the tapes, House Judiciary Committee Chairman Peter Rodino announced that his committee would "proceed full steam ahead" to organize an inquiry. On the same day, Carl Albert expressed his determination that the House must lay "this thing to rest one way or the other." In the meeting on October 30, the full House Judiciary Committee empowered Chairman Rodino to secure subpoenas without a Committee vote. Rodino made an important move thereafter: promising to consult with the Judiciary Committee's ranking Republican, Edward Hutchinson. His gesture was the first of many to foster an appearance and spirit of bipartisanship, which was vital to achieve the real purpose of the impeachment proceeding.[46]

The dominance of the Washington collective power dynamics was restored eventually.

NOTES

1. Dash, Samuel. *Chief Counsel: Inside the Ervin Committee.* (New York: Random House, 1976), 85.
2. Dash, *Chief Counsel,* 85.
3. Ervin, Sam Jr. *The Whole Truth: The Watergate Conspiracy.* (New York: Random House, 1980), 117.
4. Dash, *Chief Counsel,* 144-145.
5. Bourdieu, Pierre, and Jean-Claude Passeron. *Reproduction in Education, Society, and Culture.* Trans. Richard Nice and Tom Bottommore. (London: Sage, 1977), 7.
6. Dash, *Chief Counsel,* 88.
7. Dash, *Chief Counsel,* 89.
8. For the complete story, see Dash, *Chief Counsel,* 100.
9. Lang, Gladys Engel and Kurt Lang. *The Battle for Public Opinion—the President, the press, and the polls during Watergate.* (New York: Columbia University Press, 1983), 62.
10. *New York Times,* May 11, 17, 25, 26, 1973; *Washington Post,* May 18, 19, 1973.
11. Lang and Lang, *The Battle for Public Opinion,* 87.
12. Lang and Lang, *The Battle for Public Opinion,* 62-63.
13. Lang and Lang, *The Battle for Public Opinion,* 63-64.
14. Kutler, Stanley I. *The Wars of Watergate: The Last Crisis of Richard Nixon.* (New York: Knopf, 1990), 381.
15. McQuaid, Kim. *The Anxious Years—America in the Vietnam-Watergate era.* (New York: Basic Books, 1989), 168.

16. Lang and Lang, *The Battle for Public Opinion*, 93.
17. Bernstein, Carl and Bob Woodward. *All the President's Men*. (New York: Simon & Schuster, 1974), 176-177.
18. Bernstein and Woodward. *All the President's Men*, 177.
19. Drew, Elizabeth. *Washington Journal: the events of 1973-1974*. (New York: Random House, 1975), 60-61.
20. Dash, *Chief Counsel*, 114-115; 136-137.
21. Thompson, Fred D. *At That Point in Time: The Inside Story of the Senate Watergate Committee*. (New York: Quadrangle, 1975), 110.
22. Thompson, *At That Point in Time*, 111.
23. Dash, *Chief Counsel*, 201.
24. Dean, John W. III. *Blind Ambition: The White House Years*. (New York: Simon & Shuster, 1976), 121.
25. Dash, *Chief Counsel*, 201-202.
26. Drew, *Washington Journal*, 7.
27. Drew, *Washington Journal*, 7-8.
28. Drew, *Washington Journal*, 22-23.
29. Drew, *Washington Journal*, 23.
30. Dash, *Chief Counsel*, 207.
31. Kutler, *The Wars of Watergate*, 406.
32. White, Theodore. *Breach of Faith: The Fall of Richard Nixon*. (New York: Atheneum, 1975), 268.
33. White, *Breach of Faith*, 268-269.
34. Kutler, *The Wars of Watergate*, 410.
35. Drew, *Washington Journal*, 62.
36. Drew, *Washington Journal*, 81.
37. Kutler, *The Wars of Watergate*, 409-410; White, *Breach of Faith*, 268-269.
38. White, *Breach of Faith*, 268.
39. Kutler, *The Wars of Watergate*, 410-411; 413.
40. White, *Breach of Faith*, 268.
41. Drew, *Washington Journal*, 81-82.
42. Drew, *Washington Journal*, 81.
43. Drew, *Washington Journal*, 88.
44. White, *Breach of Faith*, 278.
45. Drew, *Washington Journal*, 100.
46. *New York Times*, Oct. 24, 31, 1973; Kutler, *The Wars of Watergate*, 412; Lang and Lang, *The Battle for Public Opinion*, 105.

Chapter Five

The Difficulty of Uncoupling Inside Washington

THE END OF THE ERVIN COMMITTEE HEARINGS

The storm after the "Saturday Night Massacre" was fading quickly. As Elizabeth Drew observed on November 6, she could see the familiar cycle: Nixon's standing suffered and went down; he then recovered, but not quite to the point where he was before. "The politicians, fingers ever to the wind, temporarily back off." After Senator Brooke called for the President's resignation, no other Republican Senators joined him. "He was left alone out on that limb." Democrats on Capitol Hill also played to opportunism. They said they did not want to appear partisan. So they were "in a holding pattern."[1]

A poll of House members in early November on how they would vote if asked to impeach the President showed that of every ten, two were ready to vote "yes," nearly four prepared to vote "no," and the rest yet undecided.[2]

Despite the ebbs and flows of the event, there was one thing consistent, and that was the lack of effective connection between Washington and the nation. The collective power dynamics in Washington could not be transformed into the national collective power in an orderly way. Many political maneuvers were needed. Such maneuvers were not without reason. Drew recorded on November 20, 1973 that not only the Republican Party was damaged badly by Watergate; both parties had lost ground in terms of public support. More and more people called themselves independents.[3]

Nixon and the Washington politicians were still together in the minds of the ordinary citizens. The uncoupling process was very difficult. For the purpose of dealing with this problem, the strategy for Washington politicians remained the same, despite the fire-storm after the "Saturday Night Massacre."

The end of the Ervin Committee Hearing demonstrated this aspect of the Washington collective power dynamics.

As the impeachment proceedings officially went "full steam ahead" after the "Saturday Night Masscre," the Senate Watergate Committee suddenly stopped publicizing further those deeper and more fundamental crimes. The public hearings of dirty tricks and illegal campaign financing never went anywhere. Dash's attempt to expand the public hearings to other areas was viewed as uncalled-for. For Dash, in addition to the Watergate break-in and cover-up, it was necessary to expose to the public the two other areas, illegal campaign financing and political dirty tricks. These two areas were included in the original design of the Senate Select Committee's investigation and they were the natural extension of the Watergate case. They were at least as important as exposing the break-in and cover-up from the legal-institutional perspective. Although Dash and his staff continued making efforts in these two areas, their political support was diminishing to virtually zero.

By November 15, Dash and his staff had called everyone on their published witness list, having produced in public hearings a capsule version of illegal and unethical campaign practices and financial contributions. But "the committee and the Washington press corps continued to demonstrate their indifference and lack of sensitivity to what I considered to be basic acts of political immorality and abuse of powers."[4] Dash gave an example to show how cold those powerful politicians were when there was a conflict between their immediate selfish pursuit of power and their institutional duty. The occurrence below clearly showed the inconsistency between the Washington collective power dynamics and the state institutional construction.

William Marumoto was an important person in the White House's so-called "responsiveness" program. According to this plan, each grant and contract in the various departments of the executive branch was to go through a final political approval to ensure that only the friends of the Nixon administration were recipients while Nixon's enemies were cut off "without a dime." As Dash wrote; "The enormity and scope of the plan, . . . made this program much more pervasive and dangerous to a free society."[5] It was true, certainly. It reflected a fundamental problem of the system and must be properly solved. The power relationship that created this kind of political favoritism must be changed. But, it received no attention at all from the press. The Senate Committee itself practically boycotted Marumoto's testimony. Everyone on the Committee displayed indifference to the shocking story. Senator Montoya shifted the issue in another direction—he blasted Marumoto's activities as an insult to American minority groups because of their focus on buying minority votes through the offer of favored deals. Senator Weicker even made a general statement supporting political favoritism bestowed by an incumbent party. Senator Baker, presiding in Ervin's absence, complimented Weicker for his statement defending the system. His remarks clearly implied that Dash had demonstrated extreme political naivete. Baker irresponsibly concluded, "the record would speak for itself." It would be clear that the record would speak for itself. But without the support of those powerful politicians, few would read it. Under such a harsh situation, Dash found it difficult to continue his work. A general morale problem spread among his staff. They developed feelings of uncertainty, which effectively blocked further investigation.[6]

At the same time, Dash's Republican counterpart used a common trick in political struggle to terminate the investigation once and for all. Here we can see, once again, the working of the collective power dynamics. Under the original Senate Resolution which created the Ervin Committee, one-third of the professional and clerical members of the Committee staff were appointees of the Republican members of the committee. This was to ensure that allegations of wrongdoing by Democrats in the presidential campaign of 1972 were adequately investigated. Dash had already assured Thompson that he would fully support his pursuit of Democratic campaign improprieties. Thompson used this opportunity, turning the Committee's investigation into a deadlock. "Okay, you boys investigate our people and if they are guilty, so be it; but in the meantime, we're going to investigate your people with no holds barred."[7] He thus pursued powerful men in the Democratic Party, like Senator Humphrey, to send a message that "once an investigation tiger is let out of the cage it is destined to rattle a lot of people before being caged again."[8] The deal among those powerful politicians was thus reached—No further action taken.

Despite the fact that the Committee requested and received two time extensions from the Senate, as well as a supplemental appropriation, there were no results from the investigation of the Rebozo fund, the milk contributions, or other areas concerning the deeply rooted political crimes committed by the Nixon administration. What had been exposed and made known across the nation was only the Watergate incident; the issues and personalities which had been debated in Congress were only Nixon as a villain and the break-in and cover-up as the sole crime. Nixon personally had been shown guilty and his administration was damaged beyond repair. The Washington collective power dynamics among powerful politicians defeated Nixon, one of their own. But the Ervin Committee's attempt to reach-out beyond Washington was not successful. Therefore, the Washington collective power dynamics reached its limit. Further action would only hurt all the people in the high political circle together with Nixon. The Committee could only play its role in a confined space.[9]

THE TAPE TRANSCRIPTS

While they put the political pressure on hold, Republican politicians, sensing both the ultimate outcome and the current power dynamics, were slowly and skillfully going through the uncoupling process between themselves and Nixon. Senator Peter Dominick, a conservative Republican from Colorado, in a speech in late October, 1973, urged Republicans to follow a more independent course from here on.[10] Even very close old friends started to leave Nixon. On October 29th, The *Washington Post* quoted John Connally as saying that the President "owed the country a better explanation for his actions than we got" on the matter of the tapes and on the matter of the firing of special Prosecutor Archibald Cox. John Connally, the heir apparent in both Nixon's mind and his heart, started distancing himself from the President now.

A familiar pattern emerged: Nixon's friends and supporters started to blame him for the split between them and Nixon—a typical blaming-loser-strategy used when uncoupling deepened and widened. Elizabeth Drew asked a Republicans Senator who had been very loyal to Nixon whether it was just a matter of time before the Republicans broke with the President. The Senator's reply was a firm "Yes". Then he explained: "I considered myself a Nixon supporter. I faulted those around Nixon—felt that they used us and then cast us aside." He believed many Republicans felt the same way. "So we have to ask ourselves, 'If there's no way out for the President, how many others should suffer?'"[11]

The interpersonal connections between Nixon and most Republicans in Congress had broken. The dynamics between them changed forever. On November 27, a moderate Republican Senator talked to Drew about the relationship between Nixon and the Republicans in Congress. According to him, "Everyone is sort of at the head-shaking stage." He said "It's got to the ridicule stage." He no longer wanted to pass on any message to the President. The healthy stage of criticism had long passed. They were on the unhealthy stage of ridicule and sarcasm. Senators all gave their opinions about what Nixon had to do to get out of trouble but they did not talk anything about what they have to do to get him out of trouble. They look at it like spectators.[12]

But not everyone moved at the same pace. In spite of the rising tide of indictments, convictions, and revelations, Barry Goldwater stayed the course through the trials of October. He supported Nixon during the period after the "Saturday Night Massacre" and blamed Cox for "getting a little far afield" in his attempt to take the president to court to obtain tapes of presidential conversations.[13] Goldwater wrote in his memoir: "There is no doubt in my mind at all that Cox took the job with the intention of destroying the President. Nixon had to fire him." "It gave every anti-Nixon journalist in the country an opportunity to attack Nixon. The stories they wrote were shrill, vengeful, and greatly exaggerated."[14]

It should be noted that Goldwater's indifference toward the "Saturday Night Massacre" was not an indication of his sensitivity to his institutional duty as a Senator. Goldwater was not loyal to Nixon as a friend, either. His real concern was Nixon's ability to hold the conservative forces together as a leader, which was measured by the collective power dynamics. Once he was sure that Nixon was no longer functional in this collective power dynamics, he was ready to abandon him. One incident pushed him make up his mind.

On December 13, 1973, Goldwater was invited to have a dinner with Nixon's family and a small group of Nixon loyalists, Pat Buchanan, Bryce Harlow, and Ray Price. Having not visited with Nixon in more than a year, Goldwater was shocked by Nixon's seeming inability to conduct himself properly. He thus knew that the impact of Watergate had severely damaged Nixon's capability to govern on his and other conservative politicians' behalf. Nixon had become a broken man. This was a turning point for Goldwater.[15]

What did this mean to him? What was he going to do? Goldwater made up his mind: "Nixon had to come clean, one way or the other." He asserted: "I sensed that in the end there would be a confrontation between us. Nixon himself had remarked that he feared only one man in Congress—Barry Goldwater. If no one in the Republican Party would stand up to Nixon, I would."[16]

The release of Nixon's tape transcripts in May, 1974, decisively changed the public sentiment and also pushed more Republican politicians to abandon Nixon. Historian Stanley Kutler commented: "The October firestorm left burning embers; the release of the tape transcripts in April and May rekindled the flames. It was another disaster."[17]

The transcripts soon appeared as a paperback book and sold widely. Newspapers reprinted excerpts, usually depicting the seamier parts of presidential conversations. The television networks offered lengthy reports on the contents of the tapes. Several re-enacted the scenes of taped conversations, using the words of the transcripts. "Expletive deleted" and so much other dirty talk had devastated Nixon among those powerful politicians because they presented a very bad image of the inside political scene to the general citizenry. For some of them, a political indictment and a political trial were becoming a necessity. The collective power dynamics further strengthened the force against Nixon and therefore accelerated the process of uncoupling.

On Capitol Hill, Barber B. Conable, Jr., of New York, the fourth-ranking Republican with enormous influence on his Republican colleagues in the House, was indignant. Conable now concluded that some way would have to be found to disassociate the Republican Party from Richard Nixon. On the

House floor and in the cloakrooms, Conable found a consensus that Nixon was a liability to the party.[18]

At first, Senate Minority leader Hugh Scott tried to skirt round the core question by issuing a one-sentence statement: "The statements I made in January seem, in my judgment, to be consistent with the full material I have read." But after reading the transcript, on May 7th, he dramatically changed his attitude. He called the edited transcripts "deplorable, disgusting, shabby, immoral."[19]

According to Woodward and Berntein, House Minority Leader John Rhodes told an aide: "I have never read such sleaziness in all my life." At a press conference later that morning, a reporter told Rhodes what Senator Scott had said. "I won't quarrel with Scott's statement," Rhodes replied. The influential Republican leaders had been talking about urging a resignation for months. "There might come a point, Rhodes and Scott had agreed, when they might have to jump ship—for the sake of their dominance."[20] On May 8, Scott received a call from George Bush, then chairman of the Republican National Committee. Bush said that he "was having trouble keeping the party professionals in line." Bush was worried and did not know what to do.[21]

As the House Judiciary Committee met on May 9 to consider the impeachment resolutions, Congressman John Anderson of Illinois, chairman of the House Republican Policy Conference, called for Nixon's resignation. John Rhodes too thought Nixon should consider that option. Even Melvin Laird, a well-connected former congressman, Nixon's former Defense Secretary and his advisor, warned his Republican friends to be "careful" and "cautious" in their support of Nixon.[22]

What was the motivation embedded in those powerful politicians' action at this moment? Elizabeth Drew had a talk with an aide to a Democratic senator. She described the deep thought of this person: "Releasing those transcripts made him more human, one of the boys," and, "Making him more human makes him more likely to be impeached."[23]

The release of those tapes with so much dirty talk in them revealed the seamy side of the operational process in Washington. It seriously tarnished the collectively shared image of those Washington politicians. More and more of them thus collectively felt embarrassed and were eager to disassociate themselves with Nixon. One of the ways they did this was to show their outrage. The entire Watergate struggle was based on the collective power dynamics among powerful politicians who tried to safeguard the collectively shared common interests already vested in them. But at the same time, they created a situation in which the entire collectivity might suffer. The release of the tape transcripts intensified the situation and made those Washington politicians feel the urgency to end the Watergate struggle as quickly as possible. Nixon became an embarrassment to all people inside the power system, especially the Republicans. He had to go in order to save everybody from further embarrassment. But, the power dynamics were complicated. Those powerful politicians had to face a crucial question: how to get rid of Nixon without hurting themselves? The key was to push the collective power dynamics further against Nixon. This was the best way to mobilize and unite more Washington politicians to join the collective force. There was much more maneuvering that needed to be done.

POWER MANEUVERING

What Democrats feared most was a partisan vote for impeachment. Fatigued as they were after carrying the battle for so long and having experienced such a great victory, they knew that if the Republicans could not join in the impeachment process, they would look bad if they were too stubborn on impeachment. Some of the Democrats who had favored impeachment passionately before started thinking whether it was worth it all anymore. Some of them even informally talked about censuring the President rather than impeaching him.[24] But they were riding on a tiger—it became impossible to turn it off even if they desired to do so. They had to figure out how to finish the task.[25]

Republicans faced another problem. They were in the same camp with Nixon and shared the same support from the same social groups. It was estimated that about twenty-five to thirty percent grass-roots Republicans who constituted a hard core. These people were the core of the party, but at the same time, they were strong Nixon supporters. Their support for the Republican Party was real, and their support for Nixon was real, too. Furthermore, they not only represented themselves in the upcoming election in November, but also exerted great influence in the party as a whole. They were well-organized among themselves and highly-motivated; they were the people who were the activists and who worked hardest in the Party. They were the people who would ring the door bells, make the phone calls, stand in the winter wind holding posters, organize and participate in rallies, and raise money for candidates. They were the people who would do all the other things that were necessary to run local campaigns.

Because of the long indoctrination of the Republican Party, this group of people regarded the press and the Congressional liberals as their true enemies. Since they also regarded Nixon as a representative of the Republican ideology, their enemies were Nixon's too. Nixon's fight was their fight. In their eyes, Nixon was only a victim of these evil people in the press and in Congress. Therefore, these hard-core people had the motivation to make life miserable for Republicans who stood against their President. Even though their numbers were only around twenty-five percent, as some people estimated, they were still a formidable force because it would not take very many of these hard-core people to give any Republican Congressman who would vote for impeachment a hard time. Two or three people at each Republican meeting would be powerful enough to shift the direction of the meeting and transform it into infighting. These party activists had not only the motivation, but also the capacity. They were a decisive grass-roots force in the Republican Party. The task the Republican politicians faced was how to separate themselves from Nixon without alienating their shared social support.

State and local Republican Party leaders across the country, such as the county chairmen, were also divided. They were not yet ready to prefer Nixon leaving office. For party politics, some of them did not like Ford as the incumbent in 1976. The moderates preferred Rockefeller and the right wing conservatives were determined to follow Reagan. Before they worked out a new leader who could balance the different factions in the Party, Nixon was still important functionally.[26]

What was the relationship between the party grass-roots and those powerful politicians in Washington? How could the Washington politicians deal with this group of citizens? It was a task of shifting the mind and heart of these grass-roots people. The task was not easy but not too difficult, either. Cohen revealed this side of the story. On March 18 Cohen talked with Elizabeth Drew. When he was asked if he had been under any pressure from the Party, he replied: "Not much." The Party state chairman and the state chairman of the Committee for the Re-Election of the President had visited him. They tried to find out how Cohen would think about this matter. Cohen made it clear that he was basing his decision on the facts. For Cohen, although the political problems on this issue for Republicans were that about twenty-five to thirty percent of the Republicans still steadfastly supported Nixon,[27] he was his own boss. The local party leaders would be under control. For whatever he was going to do "based on the facts," the local party leaders would not become a threat to his position. As to those twenty-five to thirty percent hard core Republicans, Cohen was confident that he would be able to convince them with the facts.[28]

For Cohen as an individual, it was not too difficult. It was only a matter of time until he accomplished this task. But for Republican leaders in Washington as a whole, the uncoupling process would be a little more time-consuming. They needed time to safely uncouple themselves from Nixon in order to shift the minds and hearts of all the hard core Republican grass-roots. For this purpose, they needed to unify the collective power of the Washington Republican politicians first. They had to travel some longer length. Before they achieved this goal, it might be hard to get these die-hard party loyalists in line. Soon after Rhodes, the House Republican leader, made his remarks on resignation, his office was swamped with phone calls objecting to it. Some of the callers even threatened his life. An FBI agent was sent to his office to stand guard.[29] He was also besieged by letters and telegrams. The response had been markedly pro-Nixon by about ten to one. It looked like Rhodes was now doing a great deal more than offending Nixon; he was also offending the power barons of the Republican Party and the thousands of men and women who were tied to the Republican Party as a whole and to Nixon as its leader. They were the very people who had been rewarded before and after Nixon's election.

Barry Goldwater knew how to deal with the situation. He kept publicly stating that he would not ask the president to step down. In January 1974 after he had determined he would clash with Nixon one way or another, he blamed the Democrats for "dragging" the matter out for "no better reason than to gain political advantage." Even as late as in May, Goldwater still worked to put up a more visible show of support for Nixon. Guaranteed a warm welcome, Nixon flew to Phoenix for his first public appearance since the release of the edited transcripts. The state Republican organization turned out sixteen thousand enthusiastic men and women for "a straight-out party pep rally . . . in the heart of Barry Goldwater country." Goldwater made his pledge of confidence later at a reception in his Scottsdale home.[30]

However, behind the resolute public mask was Barry Goldwater the practical politician. After he determined an inevitable confrontation with Nixon in the winter of 1973, he sensed that, in spring 1974, Nixon's chance of survival was slim. The unraveling of Nixon's defense and the potential political fallout for Republicans led him and John Rhodes, the House minority leader also from Arizona, to discuss, on several occasions, the possibility of suggesting resignation to Nixon. After all, collective interests defined by party leaders were more important than the sentiments of those hard-core party members.

> Frankly, it gets down to one question: Does the President want to see the destruction of the two-party system which will most certainly occur if he remains in office, or would he, in the interest of maintaining that system, step down? If we continue to lose elections, and there is no indication that we will not, then the politics of America will come under the domination of the labor movement, all of the radical groups who have crept in bed with government.[31]

Just as Cohen had mentioned, the strategy for Washington party leaders to shift party grass-roots' standing on the issue was to find hard facts. John Rhodes, who was threatened by his constituents, fully recognized this strategy: "The only thing to do is wait, look at the evidence."[32]

By the end of April, 1974, the Republican Party had lost the election in Michigan's Eighth Congressional District, a seat that Republicans had held for forty-two years.[33] The election outcome provided solid ground to justify the President's impeachment. It might be a way to make a case for those hard core Republicans that Nixon should be removed from office not because he did anything wrong but because he had become the liability of the Party. He hurt the collective interest of the Party as a whole. This was a sign of the direction of the collective power dynamics.

The legal preparation for the final battle was ready. The impeachment proceeding was not only up to Congress; there was also the Special Prosecutor. With the tapes and Dean's testimony, there was sufficient evidence for Jaworski to indict the President for conspiracy to obstruct justice in the Watergate investigation.

But for Jaworski, to take on the Presidency was too much for one prosecutor and a grand jury of twenty-three citizens. The Supreme Court might rule the indictment unconstitutional; besides, the President was not only an individual, he was the embodiment of the Presidency, an institution that had such an important function for the nation. But, at the same time, as the Special Prosecutor, he must prove to the nation that no person, not even the President, was above the law. The task was to find a middle ground—not to indict Nixon, but certainly not to walk away from the evidence. Jaworski wisely recognized that he personally would not take such a big responsibility. He should hand over the evidence to the elected representatives of the people, the House and the Senate, which had been assigned by the Constitution to impeach and remove a President. He wanted to throw the ball to the House Judiciary committee.

Some of the attorneys in Jaworski's office launched a full scale and often bitter debate. Their rationale was that the President's participation in the cover-up was a criminal matter, while impeachment was political. They did not feel that the House Judiciary Committee could be relied on. The Committee could find many ways to evade its responsibility. Anything could happen if the case were transformed from legal to political.

But Jaworski knew more about politics. Legal evidence and rationale alone could not replace the collective power dynamics in a power struggle in Washington. This effectiveness of the legal proceedings depended on the Washington collective power. The House Judiciary Committee was the best place to mobilize such a collective power. He would give Doar, the Committee's chief lawyer, a road map that included the tapes. All the evidence he was going to hand over to the Committee would be well-organized and complete.[34]

FURTHER AMASSING COLLECTIVE POWER INSIDE WASHINGTON

However, it was apparent that it was still premature to openly show the breakup between the party leadership and Nixon to the hard-core Republicans in the grass-roots organizations. A trail balloon was down at the end of May. Goldwater publicly broached the resignation option in a Newsweek interview and received a heavy outpouring of mail, ten-to-one in Nixon's favor.[35] Goldwater and Rhodes recognized that before these forces within Republican Party became controllable, they would have to put the abandoning of Nixon on hold. The reality was that the Washington collective power dynamics could not effectively connect to the nation. Since the power players did not feel comfortable to establish a genuine connection, their strategy was to further amass the collective power inside Washington.

John Rhodes called a meeting of the House Republican leaders. He shared his doubts with them, among them Conable, Anderson, and Robert Michel, chairman of the House Republican Campaign Committee.

Rhodes reminded these Republican leaders that many of them, like himself, would face a tough reelection campaign in November. They could not afford to alienate their power base back home. Also, the general situation for Republicans was awful. There was financial crisis, as well as a personnel crisis. George Bush was likely to resign as the party Chairman. The White House, under current circumstances, would have difficulty pursuing anybody of stature to take his place. Rhodes made it clear that for Republicans in Congress it would not be wise to declare themselves independent of the Republican in the White House right at this critical time.

John Anderson disagreed. According to him, it was time for leadership. Those die-hard Nixon loyalists were only a minority in the party and they could not determine the future of the party. The party leadership should not bend to them.

In the end, the leaders of these Republican Congressmen decided to quietly poll the House Republicans. The result was clear: an overwhelming majority of House Republicans did not want to involve themselves in the impeachment mess until after the November election. They did not want their leaders to force a resignation, either.[36] What they most needed was the party unity and, at the same time, most feared was the premature publicity of a split within the party while those hard-core Republicans were still not "well-educated about the facts." The decision was thus reached: follow the money by following the people who could get money for you; follow the vote by following the people who could get votes for you.

Would these Republican politicians really follow these hard-core party loyalists? No. What they really wanted to follow was the Washington collective power dynamics. The only task was to convince these party grass-roots and justify to these people what they had done and what they were going to do. As New York congressman Fish put it: "What these political animals are concerned with is not so much the way it's going to end up as how they're going to justify it."[37] From these words, it was clear that these citizens' representatives were not set out to do what citizens wanted them to do; they could do whatever they wanted as long as they could justify their action to their specific constituents.

Congressman Railsback also made such a point very clearly. He said that he took a survey recently. A very small percentage favored impeachment. Only twenty-four or twenty-five percent were for impeachment and sixty-seven percent were against. What did this result tell him? Like Fish, Railsback put it very clearly, he would not follow his constituents. It was not his constituents' opinion that changed him, rather, he would change their opinion. So the survey result only meant, "I'd better know what I'm talking about if I vote for impeachment."[38]

It was clear here that the relationship between those congressmen and their constituents was not an institutionalized democratic one. It was commonly regarded that, to be reelected, members must please their constituents. They could best accomplish this task by working in Congress to advance those interests as defined by local people. Their constituents certainly thought so. A Harris survey indicated that about twice as many voters said that when a legislator saw a conflict between "what the voters think best" and "what he thinks best," he or she should obey the voters. Additional studies confirmed these findings about this popular myth.[39]

However, in the Watergate investigation and impeachment process, ultimately, the Representatives and Senators did not need to follow their constituents. Rather than trying to represent their constituents' minds and hearts, these people searched for a way to shift their constituents' minds and hearts. In the end, the question became how they got their constituents to accept what they were going to do. If they could manipulate their constituents under control, they would do it; otherwise, they would wait for some time then try again in another way.

At that critical point in the impeachment process, the Washington political leaders sensed the necessity to see the process through. As a Washington insider analyzed: "The vindication of the system has become an end in itself." The reason was the difficulty of "dealing with two hundred million people who live by symbols and myths." What came out of the Watergate process would be vital to maintain these symbols and myths.[40]

But since their connection to their constituents was superficial, this was not as easy a task as it was first thought it would be, and they had a lot of work to do before it finally ended. John Rhodes, after changing his position by feeling his unreadiness to deal with the twenty-five percent Republican hardcore, put out a rationale in mid-June. Trying to change his constituents' opinion, he said that if the President defied the Supreme Court he "probably could not survive" impeachment. Here, he used the law as symbol and the Supreme Court as its carrier to change his constituents.⁴¹

However, Rhodes' comment was only a foreshadowing of the story in the future. At that moment by early June, the time had not come yet. The Washington political leaders still had to carry a heavy burden and walk down the road for a while. Inwardly eager to drive Nixon out of office, the politicians outwardly softened their position, again. For Republicans, the key here was whether they could find timely justification regardless of whether this "thing" of impeachment should happen or not. An important Republican revealed what was in these political leaders' minds. He said that there was a one-hundred-and-eighty-degree difference between wishing the President out of office and voting to impeach him. If he voted to impeach, he would have to have sound reasons to do so in order to justify his action. If he voted against it, he could easily say that the evidence was not sufficient and then move on to talking about other issues.⁴² It would be clear that before their justification was ready, most of the Republican members and some of the Southern Democrats on the Judiciary Committee would remain publicly undecided. Since this was supposed be collective power, the dynamics must be collective instead of individual. The more eagerly they inwardly wanted Nixon out, the more partisan they would be outwardly. The whole thing was to show their "objectivity and fair-mindedness" to their hard-core constituents before the rationale and justification were worked out among themselves.

In June, Henry Kissinger successfully negotiated a disengagement settlement between Syria and Israel. Nixon used this opportunity for a "triumphal tour through the Middle East." Then he visited the Soviet Union. At the time when the Judiciary Committee was meeting behind closed doors, it appeared that Nixon's chances of surviving Watergate were improved. Ratings of his job performance gained slightly. More significant, there were also signs of impeachment weariness. On June 21–24, a Gallup poll showed that a majority of Americans believed there had been "too much media coverage" of Watergate. Though polls continued to show that the public opinion supported the Committee's quest for the release of the tapes and other evidence, more and more people started doubting its ability to judge the case fairly. Thus, opposition to impeachment appeared to be gaining some ground during the month before the formal debate began.⁴³ It appeared that some measures must be taken to strengthen the collective power in Washington in order to finishing the case.

NOTES

1. Drew, Elizabeth. *Washington Journal: the events of 1973–1974.* (New York: Random House, 1975), 105.

2. Lang, Gladys Engel and Kurt Lang. *The Battle for Public Opinion—the President, the press, and the polls during Watergate*. (New York: Columbia University Press, 1983), 121.
3. Drew, *Washington Journal*, 124.
4. Dash, Samuel. *Chief Counsel: Inside the Ervin Committee*. (New York: Random House, 1976), 214.
5. Dash, *Chief Counsel*, 214.
6. Dash, *Chief Counsel*, 214–215.
7. Thompson, Fred D. *At That Point in Time: The Inside Story of the Senate Watergate Committee*. (New York: Quadrangle, 1975), 206.
8. Thompson, *At That Point in Time*, 206.
9. Thompson, *At That Point in Time*, 249.
10. Drew, *Washington Journal*, 100.
11. Drew, *Washington Journal*, 112; 113.
12. Drew, *Washington Journal*, 133–134.
13. Goldberg, Robert Alan. *Barry Goldwater*. (New Haven, CT.: Yale University Press, 1995), 277–278.
14. Goldwater, Barry M. *With No Apologies—the personal and political memoirs of United States Senator Barry M. Goldwater*. (New York: William Morrow, 1979), 260.
15. Goldberg, *Barry Goldwater*, 278–279.
16. Goldberg, *Barry Goldwater*, 271.
17. Kutler, Stanley I. *The Wars of Watergate: The Last Crisis of Richard Nixon*. (New York: Knopf, 1990), 453.
18. Woodward, Bob and Carl Bernstein. *The Final Days*. (New York: Simon & Schuster, 1976), 157.
19. Kutler, *The Wars of Watergate*, 453–454.
20. Woodward and Bernstein. *The Final Days*, 155–156.
21. Woodward and Bernstein. *The Final Days*, 159.
22. Kutler, *The Wars of Watergate*, 455–456.
23. Drew, *Washington Journal*, 265.
24. Drew, *Washington Journal*, 313.
25. Drew, *Washington Journal*, 375–376.
26. Drew, *Washington Journal*, 313.
27. Drew, *Washington Journal*, 203.
28. Drew, *Washington Journal*, 203.
29. Woodward and Bernstein. *The Final Days*, 162.
30. Goldberg, *Barry Goldwater*, 280–281.
31. Goldberg, *Barry Goldwater*, 281.
32. Drew, *Washington Journal*, 222.
33. *Washington Post*, April 20, 1974.
34. Woodward and Bernstein. *The Final Days*, 116–119.
35. Goldberg, *Barry Goldwater*, 281.
36. Woodward and Bernstein. *The Final Days*, 176–177.
37. Drew, *Washington Journal*, 282.

38. Drew, *Washington Journal,* 296.
39. Davidson, Roger H. and Walter J. Oleszek. *Congress and Its Members.* 7th ed. (Washington, D.C.: CQ Press, 2000), 103.
40. Drew, *Washington Journal,* 289.
41. Drew, *Washington Journal,* 292.
42. Drew, *Washington Journal,* 313.
43. Lang and Lang. *The Battle for Public Opinion,* 171.

Chapter Six

The Final Advancement of the Washington Collective Power

REFRAMING: THE SENATE SELECT COMMITTEE'S FINAL REPORT

On June 27, 1974, the Senate Select Committee struck another blow to the Nixon presidency, the last one in its almost one-and-half year duration, and thus ended its splendid history. This blow was timely; it reframed the Watergate affair and thus provided the much needed rationale and justification for the impeachment proceedings. The new frame effectively unified those powerful politicians. The Committee unanimously approved a final report of 1094 pages and filed it with the Clerk of the Senate. Without drawing ultimate conclusions about the current impeachment, the report was one to draw a picture that is a great likeness without writing under it "This is a horse."[1]

By reframing the Watergate affair, the report pointed out that the Watergate break-in had to be seen in the context of other White House activities. The core of these activities was abuse of power. By centering on the abuse of power, the report thus exposed facts like: extensive intelligence-gathering by the Administration, beginning soon after Nixon's inauguration in 1969; the Huston plan and "The Plumbers"; the use of the IRS, the FBI, and the CIA for political purposes—the IRS was "a preferred target of the White House staff in its attempts to politicize independent agencies"; the "Responsiveness Program," in which there was an attempt to shape the activities of departments and agencies in ways that would help Nixon's reelection; the misuse of large amounts of money and illegal campaign finance such as the money from the milk industry. Based upon these facts, the report raised a question that would be crucial to the impeachment—whether the 1972 election was genuine. The implication was clear—Nixon's mandate came from his overwhelming victory in the presidential race in 1972; if the election itself was not genuine but only a product of Nixon's abuse of power, the Nixon presidency would have no legitimacy at all. His impeachment would be justified from the deepest roots. In this way, the report provided a minimum denominator to unify Democrats and Republicans on the House Judiciary Committee.

The rationale for a justification had therefore been completed. The collective power dynamics had been energized onto a new stage. A congressman said: "It all just hit this week. . . . Especially for the conservatives: the idea of going to the IRS with a list of three hundred names of McGovern supporters and others and saying 'Fry these people'—man, that's hard to swallow."[2]

It seemed puzzling that House members were suddenly expressing so much concern about the IRS list. This list had been known about for some time. Why did the concern start at this moment? The only explanation would be the significance of reframing. Because of this reframing of the Watergate affair, the IRS list became a vital piece among so many pieces of evidences in the whole puzzle in terms of justifying the impeachment proceedings. Besides obstruction of justice, it proved Nixon's abuse of power—the danger of him staying in office became more real and threatening.

Congressman Anderson confirmed this point:

> something that caught fire—that came up quickly—was the theory of abuse of power. It was just amazing to me how the members grasped at it as an impeachable offense. They clearly thought that the part about the IRS was salable back home. The IRS as 'the jackboot of the federal government.' The idea of the abuse of power just emerged. The media hadn't built it up. Now the members are reinforcing each other. . . . The climate just built up.[3]

Mann, one of the crucial members on the Judiciary Committee, made it clear that the abuse of power was an important issue that moved the impeachment process when seven Committee members—Republicans and Southern Democrats—decided to act together bipartisanly to form a crucial coalition, "it became quickly apparent at that meeting that we were agreed on two propositions—one was obstruction of justice and the other was abuse of power."[4] It was clear how important the reframing of the Senate Watergate Committee's final report was for the vital steps of the impeachment process—the formation of the "fragile coalition" in the House Judiciary Committee.

"FRAGILE COALITION"

July 24th was the day when the House Judiciary Committee scheduled the opening of its televised final deliberation on impeachment. The closer the Judiciary Committee came to the opening of its public debate, the greater was the concern of all members with the appearance of fairness. Chairman Peter Rodino had repeatedly warned that it would be a national disaster if the Committee's inquiry were to degenerate into a partisan confrontation.[5]

At the same time, by July 24, Rhodes and House Whip Leslie Arends of Illinois advised Republicans "to keep their own counsel" until all evidence was in and arguments concluded.[6] The House Republican leadership understood the time had come.

One day before the nationally televised spectacle was about to begin, a truly dramatic development unfolded behind the scenes. The House Judiciary Committee finally gained their crucial bipartisan coalition. Several months' careful cultivation and intensive labor by Chairman Rodino and his troops finally bore fruit: some Republicans and Southern Democrats were going to go along with the Democratic majority to vote for impeachment. This would be a clear indication of the strength and direction of the collective power dynamics in Washington.

This group was known popularly as the "fragile coalition." It was an informal organization, an interpersonal network driven by the Washington collective power dynamics. At the final stage of the impeachment process, this informal body played a more important role than formal institutional arrangements. Stanley Kutler did background research on these seven members of the coalition.

First of all, the seven Congressmen of the "fragile coalition" came from districts that had delivered impressive majorities, as high as 80% with the lowest 62%, for Richard Nixon in 1972.[7]

Although these seven men had individual characteristics, all of them were on similar paths to their decisions. All stressed the weight of evidence. It would be interesting to know that after so many exposures, they were still searching for evidence. They were not trying to convince themselves, as they stated clearly. "Evidence" was the means for them to evaluate the Washington power dynamics in order for them to better position themselves. Were they trying to find new evidence to convince their constituents? The answer would be no. The fact was that what they needed was not evidence in a legal sense; they needed a coherent Washington framing of the event to shape and reshape the evidence everybody already knew. They needed such a framing to change the minds and hearts of their constituents. They, in fact, paid little attention to their constituents back home.

As to the four Republican members, William Cohen was the first one to make up his mind. He had joined the Democrats on several key votes before the coalition took shape. Although Cohen confronted significant opposition in his district, and he realized that a majority of his constituents opposed impeachment, he had been driven by the power dynamics in the Republican Party. He and Elliot Richardson lived near each other and had a thriving friendship. Both of them were moderates in the Republican Party, which was much more close to Rockfeller than to Nixon. Cohen had clashed with the Republican leadership as far back as Ford's confirmation hearings.[8]

Caldwell Butler of Virginia made up his mind relatively easily. He was an exception because he did not really care whether he would be re-elected or not. He told a friend "The job's not that good anyway." He personally did not like Nixon and considered him "cold-blooded."[9]

Hamilton Fish's Hudson River Valley constituents had been a long-time conservative-Republican bastion. His father, Hamilton Fish, Sr., a former Congressman in the 1930s and 1940s, was a die-hard Nixon supporter. But Fish did not follow his father. He was closer to the Washington collective power and more sensitive to the power dynamics; Fish believed that impeachment existed as a real possibility. It could not be decided by "a poll and popular sentiment." Impeachment involved a "very, very defined constitutional responsibility" that popularity or partisanship could not affect. But unlike Cohen, Fish had no desire to operate on his own: "I was perfectly willing to confess that I did want company."[10] He subjected himself to the collective power in Washington. When the power came, his mind was made up.

Tom Railsback of Illinois had significant personal and political ties to Nixon. To some extent, he owed Nixon his seat. Railsback personally liked Nixon. But his major concern was his standing in the Republican Party. Railsback recalled that the inquiry was not "all roses," that at times it became "very antagonistic," "disputatious," and "impassionate." One GOP committee staff member remembered that many Republicans disliked Railsback. They thought that he was a "weak man." Railsback tried very hard to find a middle ground on which to stand. He thus told Republican National Committee Chairman George Bush that he would support the President if he produced the requested materials to the Committee; he also told Julie Nixon Eisenhower the same words. In the end, he justified his decision for impeachment by bitterly recalling that the only reply to his words was more stonewalling.[11] Railsback's case showed that the collective power inside the Republican Party drove Railsback's decision-making process.

Among the three Democrats, James Mann represented a district in South Carolina that was dominated by textile-management executives. His power base back home was very conservative while the AFL-CIO rated him zero. Mann played a key role in the coalition. Although he was conscious of Nixon's strong support in his district and he remained publicly undecided until early July, he sensed the collective power dynamics in Washington through his close relationship with John Doar, the chief council for the House Judiciary Committee. The repeated discussions with Doar about Doar's detailed materials relieved his burden about uncoupling with Nixon. It had become more and more clear to him that collective power dynamics inside the Committee were definitely against Nixon. It would be safe to vote for impeachment in a collective sentiment like that.[12]

For Walter Flowers, who represented Alabama's Seventh District, one that contained the largest percentage of blacks in the state, it was the collective power of the Democratic Party that pushed him to decide for impeachment. He constantly voted with the liberal wing in his party when they needed him. He made his decision in March when he heard Nixon on tape entertaining Dean's idea about the cover-up. He felt the conversation "disgusting" and decided to go with the rest of the Party.[13]

Ray Thornton of Arizona also represented his state's largest concentration of blacks. In 1973, the Americans for Democratic Action gave him a 48-percent rating. It was Nixon's abuse of power that changed his mind. He believed that Nixon had damaged the Washington community as a whole. At the same time, he was not worried about the opposition of his constituency because he believed that they trusted him to make a "serious and judicious" decision.[14]

The networking force also worked here. The comfortable personal relationships played a role. Mann described how they got together. Flower and Railsback were best friends. After talking with Cohen and Mann, Flower called a meeting of these seven swing members in Railsback's office. They were all interested in further meetings. "We met, . . . and it was very comfortable."[15]

As a result, as Kutler observed, the truly bipartisan coalition was in a position to determine the nature and outcome of the impeachment hearings.[16]

THE SUPREME COURT RULING ON EXECUTIVE PRIVILEGE

On July 24, The Supreme Court of the United States ruled 8-0 that Nixon must, despite his claim of executive privilege, turn over his tapes to Judge Sirica. Institutionally speaking, the Supreme Court played a formalistic function. People regarded this court as the last guarantor of the system when other remedies fail. In the Watergate case, the Supreme Court was supposed to deal only with Nixon's claims of executive privilege to keep his tapes from the Special Prosecutor. Although legally the Court's decision was not framed as deciding Nixon's ultimate fate, the reality was plainly clear. In a fierce political power struggle, the Court, to a large extent, was perceived as the only government institution serving as disinterested constitutional arbiters. Despite the political bearing of the Court's role, the Justices were, in the eyes of most ordinary citizens, above politics and partisan infighting.

However, from the time of John Marshall, the Court frequently has fallen afoul of particular interests; its authority rose and fell following the Washington collective power dynamics. The Court at that time was known as the "Burger Court". Chief Justice Warren Burger was appointed by Nixon in 1969. Nixon also appointed three other justices on the Court.

In fact, the nomination and confirmation processes were more contentious. Presidents, facing the massive lobbying and public relations campaigns for or against judicial nominees, made enormous efforts using their institutional and networking power to gain momentum in the collective power dynamics.

The Nixon administration made a good example of power playing for the purpose of successfully navigating through the collective power dynamics. Since 1970 the Office of Public Liaison was established in the White House. By using such an institutional mechanism for mobilizing support, Nixon further highlighted the factor of power in the nomination process. He was eager to use the selection process to gain the upper hand in the Washington collective power dynamics.

There were two institutional establishments in the Nixon White House specializing in mobilizing social support. The first was the Office of Political Affairs headed by Harry Dent and later, the Office of Public Liaison was created. The first director was Charles Colson. Both of these two offices made enormous political efforts in the process of Supreme Court justice nomination. As Maltese recorded, in the Haynsworth nomination, Dent had a nine-page list of contacts to put pressure on target senators. He also mobilized organizations like state Republican organizations and other groups such as Young Republicans and Young Americans for Freedom to support Haynsworth. Colson did the same:

> Colson's handwritten notes indicate the following activity in support of Rehnquist and Powell:
> Calls: 1) Prominent attorneys, 2) Bar Association Leaders, 3) Republican Governors, 4) Party Officials, 5) friendly Editors & Broadcasters, 6) Columnists, 7) Loyalists, 8) Judges, 9) Hill. Group mobilization: 1) Chamber [of commerce], 2) NAM [National Association of Manufacturers], 3) NAHB [National Association of Home Builders], 4) Police Chief, 5) firefighters, 6) VFW [Veterans of Foreign Wars]. [Pat] Buchanan with conservative groups.[17]

The enormous political efforts in the nomination process clearly revealed the political nature of the Supreme Court. It was an inseparable part of the Washington collective power and subject to its dynamics. Chief Justice Burger's closeness to Nixon and the Administration was well known. Similar to Abe Fortas' case in the Johnson presidency, Burger's nomination was suspected as cronyism. The White House gossip in 1973 and 1974 reported that

Burger "had assured the President that the tapes would not be taken away." John Ehrlichman reported in 1971 that Burger had "met periodically" with the President, Mitchell, and himself "to discuss issues of the day and to join a general discussion of current events."[18] Just after the Court took the tapes case in 1974, the *Washington Post* disclosed correspondence between Burger and John Mitchell, indicating a close, "confidential" relationship between the Chief Justice and the Administration.[19]

On the other hand, Justice William O. Douglas did not like Nixon. More than a year before the Watergate case reached the Supreme Court in May 1973, Douglas was using his personal networks to "get to the bottom of the story" about some of Nixon's aides' criminal actions in California. He quickly got the response from his friends (like Palmer Hoyt—former owner of the Denver Post; James Carter—a sitting U.S. Court of Appeals judge for the Ninth Circuit; Roger Kent—a prominent San Francisco attorney) for him to demonstrate that "Our Hero [Nixon] was not the victim of unsuspected associates. He knew his way around without help." Considering the fact that Nixon and Mitchell were very active and instrumental in the impeachment proceedings in Congress against Douglas in 1970, it was easy to understand Douglas' informal legal activism against Nixon.[20]

On the surface, people might assume the Justices on the Court, with such diversified ideological backgrounds, should have hardly reached unanimity, especially when they were dealing with a complicated constitutional issue such as executive privilege. A divided ruling would be more real in terms of these Justices' independent judgment based on their authentic legalistic philosophy. The unanimity could only be explained by the unique political situation and the collective power dynamics they were collectively experiencing. It was no doubt that the political situation and the overwhelming power of the collective force in Washington effectively united the seemingly fractionalized Court. Nixon was on his deathbed politically. His situation made the Court ruling easy. What else could people expect under the circumstances at that moment? It was only natural that even Burger would want to appear independent.

St. Clair, Nixon's lawyer, represented Nixon before the Court. But he failed to convince the Justices. Watergate Special Prosecutor Jaworski and his assistant Lacovara successfully persuaded the Court on the illegality of Nixon's claim of executive privilege in a criminal investigation. All the arguments were on strict legal terms. However, as Justice Rehniquist had noted, the Justices did not live in a vacuum. Beyond doubt, the Watergate issue was the all-consuming political dilemma of the year. Watergate had inevitably captured their attention. The Watergate affair had been a frequent topic of conversations among the Justices and their clerks. The Justices and their clerks watched and listened to the Senate Select Committee hearings, together with all the others in the nation.[21] They could feel the power sliding away from Nixon. The daily revelation of the Administration's wrongdoings, some of them criminal actions, would tell the Justices and their clerks how serious the case was both in terms of politics and in terms of law. As they were trying to absorb the legal argument between Jaworski and St. Clair, they would, at the same time, sort out those materials and, especially, the general feelings they had absorbed in the previous Watergate revelations since the incident began. It was clear that the Justices "were very aware of the politics of the Watergate litigation and of the potential impact a definitive institutional judgment of the Court would have on the resolution of this dilemma." The Justices knew that the "Court's "head rush" into the controversy was a critical factor in the ultimate resolution of the societal and constitutional crisis." The Court decided to bypass the Court of Appeals, a sign of asserting itself as in a position to "clarify the Watergate mess" (Justice Douglas) in a timely fashion before a crippled presidency could cause too much damage to the governance system.[22]

In the end, Brennan and the others certainly had the input they had wanted all along; meanwhile, Burger alone had his name on an opinion that united the Court: the President must surrender the tapes. The Supreme Court finally played its institutional role but it was driven by the collective power dynamics among Justices themselves and between them and outside political leaders. It was these collective power dynamics, rather than the rational and institutional constructions, that produced the final ruling.

Nixon lost the last legal ground. As soon as his tapes were surrendered, the smoking gun would be visible to the public and the choice for him would become obvious.

THE TELEVISED DEBATE

On July 30, as the House Judiciary Committee debate ended, and the Nielsen Company informed White House aides that the debate had an estimated audience of 35-40 million—extraordinary high numbers.[23] With so many people watching the live coverage, how significant was it? If there was no live coverage of the impeachment proceedings or it were not conducted the way it was, would the Watergate affair have ended as it did? The answer must be "no."

As it was originally designed, the debate was for promoting a bipartisan image. From the very beginning, all members on the Committee, members of Congress, and even the general public had been made aware by Rodino that the appearance of fairness was at least as important as the actuality. Rodino and his staff were keenly aware of the need to make effective use of the media to carry the Washington collective power to the public.

For this purpose, they tightly controlled the flow of information for fear of an omnipresent bystander public. All the controversy and differences within the Committee were fully resolved internally before they were presented at the sight of the public. For the Committee to control the flow of official information to the press, they set up a sole link between the staff and the world outside. Francis O'Brien, Rodino's administrative assistant, held briefings every morning at nine o'clock. He was the only person who could provide official information.[24]

The telecasts changed few opinions about Nixon's legal culpability in the Watergate affair. Most people were convinced Nixon was guilty before the debate. However, more and more people began to accept the necessity for impeachment. What the televised debate had done was to legitimate the decision made by the Washington collective power to oust Nixon from the Presidency. Though the President was never actually impeached or tried by the Senate, the results were, in the eyes of most citizens, as if all legitimated legal process had run their full course. It had become more difficult for anyone to make a convincing case that Nixon had been denied due process and was being ousted from office in a political coup d'etat. The public was convinced that impeachment was fair and judicial, rather than a partisan political process. Whatever one's sentiments about Nixon and the impeachment, the prevailing view was that the televised proceedings had conveyed an image of congressional conscientiousness, intelligence, and fair-mindedness. Those images nourished a public confidence that legitimized the eventual outcome of events.[25] A Louis Harris poll taken on August 2, a week after the first vote, showed public opinion favoring impeachment 66-27 percent. Pro-impeachment sentiment had risen 13 percent in one week.[26]

Even members of the "fragile coalition" who faced the task of effectively convincing their constituents back home found the task not too difficult after all. With unity among themselves, they used the televised debate as an extraordinary opportunity. As a result, those at home responded respectably. From the mail the members received from the people back home, they knew their constituents were encouraging them to continue what they were doing. The mail showed them that it was becoming more respectable to vote their way rather than to bow to constituents' opinions. Most of their constituents "seemed to be taking a special pride after they had seen them on TV delivering such eloquent and lofty sentiments."[27]

The success in the Judiciary Committee in terms of unifying themselves and their constituents greatly encouraged the House as a whole. The collective power for impeachment had greatly strengthened. As John Anderson, chairman of the House Republican conference, asserted: "The Judiciary

Committee proceedings gave the Congress a much-needed lift. . . . members began to gather in little knots in the cloakroom and on the floor and say, 'He's had it'."[28]

An obvious question would be: "why and under what condition did the televised debate have positive impact on the general citizenry to legitimate the Presidential impeachment?" Clearly a causal relationship between the televised debate and legitimation is not universal, since the televised debate in the Clinton impeachment only served to delegitimate the process. The answer would likely be: It was important that the discordant tone in congressional politics made a difference in the two impeachment battles. The reason the Washington collective power achieved such a feat was the unity among Washington political leaders. The unified Washington collective power laid down a very solid foundation for such a success. As Peterson points out, in 1974, when Congress began proceedings against Nixon prior to his resignation, only 37 percent of the roll-call votes in Congress were party-unity votes, i,e., a majority of one party voting against a majority of the other party. Republicans and Democrats sided with their respective parties on just greater than 60 percent of recorded votes overall. When the House Judiciary Committee voted on the articles of impeachment against Richard Nixon, one article attracted more than 40 percent of the Republicans on the Committee. In 1998, on the other hand, party-unity votes constituted 56 percent of the total, and members voted faithfully with their parties approximately 85 percent of the time. In the House, the two enacted articles to impeach Clinton passed on the floor with nearly straight party-line votes (one pitted 98 percent of Republicans in favor against 98 percent of Democrats opposed). Clinton's acquittal in the Senate also basically followed party-line votes with all the Democrats on the Clinton side.[29]

Therefore, the condition that could legitimate the impeachment process in a televised hearing was the strength of the Washington collective power—whether Washington political leaders acted as a whole or they just showed their division to the public. In the case of Nixon impeachment, the core of the impeachment process from its planning to organizing was focused on bi-partisanship. Every step was a painstakingly staged bi-partisan effort before, during, and right after the televised debate. The collective power dynamics made it possible that the dominating tone and content were very clear to the general citizenry. On the contrary, in the case of Clinton impeachment, the Washington collective power dynamics worked in another direction. The Washington political leaders were badly divided. There was no dominating tone or content in the televised debate. Rather than creating, shaping, and transforming ordinary citizens' mind and heart, those powerful politicians divided into two well-matched camps with two conflicting voices competing for ordinary citizens' attention and support. This left much more space for ordinary citizens to make up their own minds; in addition, this kind of behavior projected a very bad image.

The framing and reframing processes of these two cases might help us to further understand the contrast between the Nixon impeachment, when there was unity and the Clinton case, when the division was so pronounced. These processes would highlight how the Washington collective nerve reacted to the different offenses by these two Presidents and how the collective power dynamics developed. When Watergate was framed as break-in, the powerful politicians were not united; when it was framed as cover-up, some more powerful politicians joined in, but still, they were not united; only when this case was framed as abuse of power and this frame became widely accepted, did the majority of powerful politicians finally unite. As to the Clinton case, although there were several legal litigations under investigation, almost all of them were private matters, except the Filegate—the FBI files on many Republican heavy-weights found in the White House—which had some connotation of abuse of power, but it was soon legally cleared. No matter how Clinton's opponents framed these cases, they would have a hard time stimulating a sense of threat to the Washington collective power in general. The Monica affair could only be framed, to the ultimate extreme, as perjury and obstruction of justice. But so what? Lying about a consensual sexual relationship or trying to obstruct others from knowing such a relationship in a legal investigation might be "illegal." But nobody's share of power in Washington would be hurt in anyway by such an "illegal" behavior. So why bother to politically risk so much to unite?

Framing and reframing would be indicators of the substantive collective power dynamics. There were many rival political networks within and between these two major political parties. They did not usually unite unless something truly threatening was happening. What Nixon did was truly threatening to the Washington collective power as a whole and to many powerful political leaders as individuals. Those powerful politicians would not allow a precedent to serve as an example and to justify future presidents' such violations, even though Nixon had already lost the capacity to do so at the time when impeachment was under way. On the contrary, the Clinton case could not in any way amount to even a slight threat to the collective power and individual share of power in Washington.

The carefully rehearsed and staged contents of the debate on impeachment articles also highlighted the underlying theme of the Washington collective power dynamics. There was no doubt that for the members of the House Judiciary Committee, the question was how to transform the words of the document into political power. That is, how to play the power game in order to gain more power in Washington, and then in the nation. That was exactly what the House Judiciary Committee's deliberation did. Since the source of power for the thirty-eight members of the House Judiciary Committee was not their constituents—they had power in their possession before they faced the problem of how to convince their constituents—the members of the Judiciary Committee did not need to claim power by claiming to represent their constituents; they had found something else to represent—they represented an idea. This idea would be an indicator of the Washington power dynamics.

The idea they chose was "the rule of law." This was their final frame of the event. How could we understand the fact that they chose "the rule of law" as the final frame instead of others like "the public trust?" It is clear that the violation of law was not uncommon to Presidents. LaRue took Abraham Lincoln as a good example. Lincoln's many actions were unlawful. LaRue quoted James Randall's conclusion in his book *Constitutional Problems under Lincoln*,

> He carries his executive authority to the extent of freeing the slaves by proclamation, setting up a whole scheme of state-making for the purpose of reconstruction, suspending the habeas corpus privilege, proclaiming martial law, enlarging the army and navy beyond the limits fixed by existing law, and spending public money without congressional appropriation.[30]

However, no one has even the least doubt that Lincoln is the most highly regarded President in American history who is viewed "in popular conception as a great democrat, the exponent of liberty and of government by the people," although he seized "more arbitrary power than perhaps any other President" in American history.[31]

The key was that although Lincoln seized an arbitrary power, he did not exercise that power in an arbitrary way. By comparison, Nixon seized far less power legally but used it far more arbitrarily. If we regard Lincoln as a model of democratic leadership, we would say the genuine connection between political leaders and ordinary citizens, rather than laws, should be the core of the system. Therefore, the essence of the Watergate affair was not Nixon's violation of law; it was, rather, his violation of the democratic principles. What they should have addressed was supposed to be the special relevance to impeachment in that the President was one of those things that was alienated from ordinary citizens. But the Washington political leaders did not frame the Watergate case and the Nixon violation in this way.

Here we see a deep-seated characteristic of the American political system: laws (the Constitution included) were supposed to govern the nation; the behavior codes of the Washington collective power dynamics were the real force governing Washington. A constant theme in American political history was that, since there was no mechanism for the coded Washington collective power dynamics to automatically connect Washington to the nation, laws had to be utilized in order to legitimize those Washington codes. Many political activities centered on this task. The thirty-eight Committee members' final frame about the Watergate event highlighted this point.

The Washington collective power dynamics had already pushed the event to this stage. The key issue had become how to accomplish the reach-out to the nation. The only way for them to accomplish this task was to transform the Washington codes into national laws. The nature of the system dictated that the connection they were trying to build between Washington and the nation would be a rather superficial one because, after all, laws were only the means rather than the ends. The function of laws would only be providing the standard of judgment rather than becoming the end in and of itself. Since these representatives were focused on transforming the Washington collective codes into laws, they cared little about the content issue. They therefore did not have the vision and the means to build the genuine and solid connection between Washington and the nation, between themselves and the citizens in general. They could not focus their frame on those ways that posed a fundamental danger to democracy. The only remedy to the limitation of the Washington collective power dynamics would be citizens' involvement and participation, but they could not envision or felt uncomfortable about such a construction. As LaRue observed:

> As I read the debates, this theory of democratic accountability was offered in support of Article III, but the Thornton amendment, which passed, seems to reject this theory. Consequently, our representatives did not seem most interested in strengthening democracy, and thus they would not describe the Watergate affair as a threat to democracy, but as involving something else.[32]
>
> When we see how Article III, the subpoena article, was first amended and then passed only narrowly, we can see that the topics of power, the structure of government, the theory of democracy, and citizen participation in government were topics with which the committee members felt uncomfortable. For me, this is regrettable.[33]

The first article of impeachment, which charged Nixon with obstruction of justice, passed in the Judiciary Committee by a vote of 27-11 on July 27; the second article of impeachment, which charged Nixon with abuse of power, passed by a vote of 28-10 on July 29; By a vote of 21-17, the third and final article of impeachment, which charged Nixon with unconstitutionally defying congressional subpoenas, passed on July 30.

THE FINAL ADVANCEMENT

By the end of July, the leaders of the Republican Party had already decided to abandon Nixon once and for all. The matter was not whether but when. According to Goldwater, he discussed the situation with the two GOP minority leaders, Scott of the Senate and John Rhodes of the House. They reached a conclusion that the question at the point was not whether but when Nixon would be formally impeached.[34]

Despite its imposing legal facade, impeachment, after all, was essentially a political process. Congressman Charles E. Wiggins talked about the rationale for his die-hard support of a guilty Nixon by charging that: "The Committee was formed to impeach Richard Nixon. The decision to impeach Richard Nixon was made not in the light of television, but in the Speaker's office. That is the way decisions are made in Congress."[35]

It appeared very strange that even at the point when the House Judiciary Committee passed three articles of impeachment, Nixon still had some support from the most partisan Republicans in Congress. Why were these people so stubborn? What these people feared was not the damage done to the formally institutionalized state construction, but their own position in the Washington collective power. They feared that the Republican Party would get a label "party of Watergate" if they allowed Nixon to be impeached. Based upon this consideration of interest, they rationalized and legitimized their indignation. Hypocrisy and double standards were the charges the President's defenders hurled at his attackers. Nixon was no saint but he only did what every recent President before him had also done, and most of these Presidents were Democrats. According to the charges, Lyndon Johnson had been a thief and worse, but the Democratic congressional leaders who had known that hadn't done anything against him. Instead, they had stonewalled Republican efforts to trace millions of dollars in kickbacks and favoritism and misuse of government property. Now these same people, joined by journalists and bureaucrats and lawyers and judges, were out to get Nixon because they were "marinated in hatred" against Nixon and all he stood for. All the Democrats had done was obscured their own domestic dirty tricks by blaming Nixon (and, through him, the Republicans).[36]

Thinking in this way, some Republican members of Congress kept fighting for Nixon. However, the June 23 tape put these steadfast partisan Republicans into a very difficult situation. The collective power dynamics finally produced the evidence. On August 5, Nixon made public the transcripts of three conversations he had with Haldeman on June 23, 1972, six days after the break-in. The smoking gun was there, clearly visible. It was a clear indication of the complete defeat of Nixon. House Republicans reacted with dismay, sorrow, or anger. They had no choice. They recognized that the President had to go one way or another. The overall nature of what was going on by this point was clear enough. Nixon's remaining allies deserted him, in order to save themselves and the Republican Party. All ten House Judiciary Committee members who had voted against impeaching Nixon for anything quickly reversed their stands on the obstruction of justice charge.

Senate Republican leaders continued to meet in the afternoon of August 6. Senator Scott, the Minority Leader, presided at the meeting. Besides Barry Goldwater, there were Senators Norris Cotton of New Hampshire, Wallace Bennett of Utah, Bill Brock of Tennessee, John Tower of Texas, Jacob Javits of New York, and Robert Griffin of Michigan. They were "comrades" with Nixon. They had campaigned together and had battled their common opponents together for decades. Goldwater framed his rationale for abandoning Nixon after the "smoking gun" became public. He told the members of the policy group that "I felt the President had taken advantage of our loyalty, that I for one would never again defend him, and that it was obvious to me that if he insisted on an impeachment trial, he would be convicted. I thought the best thing he could do for the nation would be to resign." He also told Haig that Nixon would be lucky if he got twelve votes if there should be an impeachment trial in the Senate. "I have been deceived by Richard Nixon for the last time. A majority of the Republicans in the Senate share my feelings."[37]

All of the Senators at that policy meeting "believed that if Nixon had told the truth at the time, if he had condemned the overzealousness of his political operatives, the public would have accepted his explanation and forgiven him. Now it was too late."[38] This was a political, rather than a legal, judgment. This was a judgment based on evaluation of the collective power dynamics rather than on the legal and institutional constructions. This was the genuine side of their feeling and the genuine side of the Washington politics.

According to Goldwater, Nixon's crime was not what he did that violated the formal state laws, but his informal and interpersonal lies. "Throughout my years in public life I have always had reservations about Richard Nixon. Despite our long association, I never felt that I truly knew him. In the moments of tension and stress we shared, he always seemed to be too well programmed, to be carefully calculating the ultimate effect of everything he did or said."[39] "Nixon's masquerade was, however, a long and tortuous trail of deceit that plundered the generosity and goodwill of millions of Americans who wished desperately to believe that their President was not a liar. It was the manipulation and misuse of this vast American store-house of bigheartedness that history will condemn."[40]

However, as a commentator asserted: "Less commendable and certainly inconsistent is the double standard he applied—one to Agnew, who lied to him and received his support and sympathy the other to Nixon, who lied to him and was condemned by him. The wide variance in Goldwater's treatment of the two men stemmed in large part from a simple fact: Goldwater counted Agnew as a friend, but he was never able to connect personally with Nixon. Friendship, for Goldwater, could cover a multitude of sins."[41] Clearly, it was interpersonal and collective concerns, rather than moral and legal ones, that hardened those Republican leaders' mind to abandon Nixon sooner, rather than later.

The meeting of the Republican Senate leadership on August 6 decided that Goldwater alone should go to the White House and, speaking for his fellow Republicans, ask Nixon to resign. For Goldwater, it was a signal of honor from his peers. It symbolized that he regained the highest status in the Republican Party after his 1964 presidential bid. But, he was still not sure about his Republican constituents when he called his wife in that evening.

He received reassurance from his wife who surely knew better: "No, Barry, they will respect your truthfulness and honor. You do what you think is right, but don't retire. It's just not the way to leave after so many years."[42]

Nixon called in the Republican leaders on August 7. Hugh Scott, John Rhodes, and Barry Goldwater met the President and indicated to him that he had no significant support in Congress. Goldwater left the meeting with no doubt as to the outcome: the President "would resign."[43] On August 8, Nixon addressed the nation announcing his resignation. On August 9 at 12:03 P.M., President Ford was formally sworn into office. He spoke to the nation: "Our long national nightmare is over. Our Constitution works. Our great republic is a government of laws and not of men. Here, the people rule."

This historical triumph of the "people ruling" was supposed to inflame public passions. However, what was striking was the fact that there was little public reaction to this event. On November 7, 1972, Nixon was reelected President by a landslide, losing only Massachusetts and the District of Columbia. If we regard election as the most important institution in the formally institutionalized state construction, the vote would be a reflection of the "people's choice". Over the dramatic resignation less than two years later, the country was supposed to be "torn apart" by the unprecedented succession. But the country was extremely calm. Citizens in general were going on vacation, or staying home worrying about inflation. They retreated to their private lives and seemed to accept whatever the results of the Watergate saga, which seemed inevitable and natural. In fact, for a long time after the "Saturday Night Massacre," except for a very small group of people led by Rabbi Korff and Reverend Moon who demonstrated against impeachment, no one did anything for impeachment. However, according to every poll estimate, more than two of every ten Americans, and possibly as few as one in ten, were unhappy with the outcome, and even this minority, while somewhat disillusioned, accepted the resignation as inevitable and necessary. Few were bitter or vengeful. An interesting point was that despite this overwhelming positive sentiment toward impeachment and resignation, citizens seemed not to care. They seemed passive. Before the big event happened, they did not make any efforts to influence or even figure out what the politicians would or would not do. After it happened, they did not celebrate on the street or even at home. The Washington collective power prevailed. It was effective; it was good; it produced a peaceful and orderly result. But it was also by insiders only. As the Longs put it: "Even more noteworthy was the strangely muted public response. Some fifteen months of apparent polarization suddenly ended without any serious political clashes or much visible dissent, without joyful demonstrations or dancing in the streets. If there were wounds to heal, they were only surface scratches."[44] An ending like this is worth pondering.

NOTES

1. Ervin, Sam Jr. *The Whole Truth: The Watergate Conspiracy*. (New York: Random House, 1980), 272; *New York Times* and *Washington Post*, July 12, 1974.
2. Drew, Elizabeth. *Washington Journal: the events of 1973-1974*. (New York: Random House, 1975), 344.
3. Drew, *Washington Journal*, 386.
4. Drew, *Washington Journal*, 377.
5. Lang, Gladys Engel and Kurt Lang, *The Battle for Public Opinion—the President, the press, and the polls during Watergate*. (New York: Columbia University Press, 1983), 142.
6. Kutler, Stanley I. *The Wars of Watergate: The Last Crisis of Richard Nixon*. (New York: Knopf, 1990), 499.
7. Kutler, *The Wars of Watergate*, 500.
8. Kutler, *The Wars of Watergate*, 500; 502–503.
9. Kutler, *The Wars of Watergate*, 499–500; 501.
10. Kutler, *The Wars of Watergate*, 500; 503.
11. Kutler, *The Wars of Watergate*, 500; 501; 503.
12. Kutler, *The Wars of Watergate*, 499; 501–502.
13. Kutler, *The Wars of Watergate*, 499; 502.
14. Kutler, *The Wars of Watergate*, 499; 502.
15. Drew, *Washington Journal*, 377.
16. Kutler, *The Wars of Watergate*, 504.
17. Maltese, John Anthony. "The Presidency and the Judiciary." in Nelson, Michael (ed.) *The Presidency and the Political System (sixth ed.)*. (Washington, D.C.: CQ Press, 2000), 524–525.
18. Kutler, *The Wars of Watergate*, 512.

19. *Washington Post*, June 13, 1974.

20. Ball, Howard. "United States v. Nixon Reexamined: The United States Supreme Court's Self-Imposed 'Duty' to Come to Judgment on the Question of Executive Privilege." in Friedman, Leon and William F. Levantrosser (eds.) *Watergate and Afterward—the legacy of Richar M. Nixon*. (Westport, Connecticut & London: Greenwood Press, 1992), 100.

21. Rehniquist, William. *The Supreme Court* (New York: Morrow, 1987), 89–90; 94; 95.

22. Ball, Howard. "United States v. Nixon" in Friedman and Levantrosser, 103.

23. *New York Times*, Aug. 5, 1974; Kutler, *The Wars of Watergate*, 531.

24. Lang and Lang, *The Battle for Public Opinion*, 145.

25. Lang and Lang, *The Battle for Public Opinion*, 138; 172.

26. Kutler, *The Wars of Watergate*, 532.

27. Lang and Lang, *The Battle for Public Opinion*, 171.

28. Drew, *Washington Journal*, 386.

29. Peterson, Mark A. "The President and Congress." in Nelson *The Presidency and the Political System*, 500.

30. LaRue, L.H. *Political Discourse—a case study of the Watergate affair*. (Athens and London: The University of Georgia Press, 1988), 138.

31. LaRue, *Political Discourse*, 138.

32. LaRue, *Political Discourse*, 56–57.

33. LaRue, *Political Discourse*, 136.

34. Goldwater, Barry M. and Jack Casserly. *Goldwater*. (New York: Doubleday, 1988), 274.

35. Wiggins, Charles E. "Panel Discussion on Impeachment Proceedings." in Friedman and Levantrosser (eds.) *Watergate and Afterward*, 229.

36. McQuaid, Kim. *The Anxious Years—America in the Vietnam-Watergate era*. (New York: Basic Books, 1989), 273.

37. Goldwater, Barry M. *With No Apologies—the personal and political memoirs of United States Senator Barry M. Goldwater*. (New York: William Morrow, 1979), 264–265.

38. Goldwater, *With No Apologies*, 265.

39. Goldwater, *With No Apologies*, 268.

40. Goldberg, Robert Alan. *Barry Goldwater*. (New Haven, CT.: Yale University Press, 1995), 255.

41. Edwards, Lee. *Goldwater—the man who made a revolution*. (Washington D.C.: Regnery Publishing, Inc.—an Eagle Publishing Co, D.C., 1995), 393.

42. Edwards, *Goldwater*, 398; Goldwater and Casserly. *Goldwater*, 276–277.

43. Kutler, *The Wars of Watergate*, 539; Woodward, Bob and Carl Bernstein. *The Final Days*. (New York: Simon & Schuster, 1976), 391–392.

44. Lang and Lang, *The Battle for Public Opinion*, 1–2.

Conclusion: Toward a Neo-Progressivism

THE CONSERVATIVE PERSPECTIVE

The conservative ideology includes fear of anarchy and distrust of mass political participation above all. For them, the only violation of Watergate was the excessive use of power; however, the system performed very well. In a timely manner, its self-correction mechanisms punished those people who crossed the line. The way Watergate was handled reasserted the virtues of the pluralist political system. Some conservative political sociologists even claimed that the scandal itself actually constituted an improvement over previous scandals in terms of dealing with unusual political situations. Their rationale was that the necessity for Nixon Administration to cover-up was itself a measure of the improvement of the American political system. Lipset & Raab compared the political behavior in the 1920s to the political behavior of the Nixon administration:

> The backlash of the 1920s, accordingly, was marked by severe violation of democratic procedure. A restrictive and racist immigration law was passed. A General Intelligence Division was established in the Attorney General's office to investigate domestic radical activities. It gathered and indexed the histories of 200,000 people for its suspect files, while the Department of Justice conducted raids, which resulted in the arrest of 10,000 people. All this was done without benefit of supporting legislation by Congress. Then state and local governments followed suit, as did private vigilante groups which hounded prostitutes and adulterers as well as political offenders. Some were lynched; many others were tarred and feathered.[1]
>
> But the point is that the Watergate horrors were perpetrated covertly, in the dark of the night, whereas in the 1920s, the illegal activities of the government were carried out in the open, and apparently with the overwhelming approval of

the American people. In the Nixon administration, by contrast, the most elaborated operation was the cover-up, which is itself a measure of the restraining power of the cosmopolitan climate not only within the administration but in the nation at large—in, that is, the growing cosmopolitanization of the American people.[2]

Therefore, it is not necessary to establish additional institutional safeguards to prevent future Watergates. Nothing needed to be worried about at all on this front. Instead of being a lesson we should learn something from, Watergate provided a good example of the strength of the existing system. It showed that the institutionalized state system with all the procedures already in place was powerful enough to put violations like Watergate to a timely end.

What worried them most was the democratic participation of ordinary citizens, even if such actions were legal. According to Conservatives, the most serious threat to the system was the possibility of destabilizing the system with mass participation. The only lesson they drew from Watergate was that too much democratic participation would be dangerous to the political system. They therefore recommended noninvolvement of the ordinary citizens in the political process. As Samuel Huntington asserted: "The entire operation of a democratic political system usually requires some measure of apathy and noninvolvement on the part of some individuals and groups."[3] The core of their entire argument is that the Watergate scandal itself was not so important—the most concern should be placed on the stability of the political system and the focus should be safe-guarding the status quo.

THE LIBERAL PERSPECTIVE

Liberals thought that they witnessed an about-to-be horror of a totalitarian state as the Watergate scandal unfolded to the public. The totalitarian state was brought so close to reality that only by accident it was stopped. They did not view Watergate as proof that the system worked. Mintz and Cohen described this liberal point of view in detail:

> No claim that "the system worked" could be made during the actual Watergate wrongdoings. Nothing had worked to block the various subversions at their inception, and nothing had worked to impede them once under way. There came a serious of accidents—a stupid break-in at the offices of the Democratic National Committee in the Watergate Office Building, a guard vigilant enough to notice a door that, inexplicably, had been taped open; two reporters with the determination and freedom to pursue the story assiduously and alone; editors willing to back them, and a newspaper owner who resolutely backed the editors; a

federal judge who refused to countenance an inadequate investigation and prosecution, but who in refusing abused his judicial powers; and the discovery, by the staff of the Senate Select Committee on Presidential Campaign Activities (Watergate committee), that the President had recorded conversations in the Oval Office and his suite in the Executive Office Building, and on several telephones. Only after such accidents did "the system" indeed begin to work and, ultimately, force Richard Nixon to flee the White House.[4]

For them, "the system almost did not work." The dangerously lawless Nixon Administration was stopped only by a series of accidents. The system only worked by good luck and good fortune. Liberals' solution for preventing Watergate from happening again was, therefore, based on legislative reform. As Mintz and Cohen pointed out:

> What is the lesson of Watergate? . . . We cannot have a system which depends on a benign executive—or a malign one. We've got to make the Congress work. There is no alternative. And if the Congress cannot be responsible, then the whole system of representative government and free-choice government is going down the drain. . . . How the Constitution might build a "web of accountability" around all our powerful institutions is the challenge that ultimately we face.[5]
>
> There is no "Mr. Congress" to respond in kind to "Mr. President."[6]
>
> Of the three branches of government, the executive and the judicial may get away with being insulated from the citizenry, but Congress is potentially the branch most exposed to democratic demand. And so turning Congress around for the people is the most practical and immediate priority in improving the executive and judicial branches as well.[7]

To reduce the danger of a totalitarian government, they proposed such formal institutional constructions as more strict campaign financing laws, an independent counsel law, and a prohibition against CIA covert domestic operations.

THE RADICAL LEFT PERSPECTIVE

The left camp can be divided into two branches: the radical left and the critical left. The radical left argued that Watergate was not simply an incident that was against the basic spirit of the American political system. For them, Watergate was not only a conflict between men of power; it also posted the issue of legitimation for the ruling class as a whole. At this point, the radical left's criticisms differed from other criticism to the American political system.

The "Bay Area Kapitalistate Group" around James O'Connor (1974) presented this perspective. They argued that the Congress and "even the liberal press, so often credited with bringing the scandal to the full attention of the American public" helped to manage the crisis. For the Kapitalistate group, Watergate constantly threatened to turn into an indictment of American "democracy" as a whole. Nixon was only a scapegoat for others to divert attention from fundamental structural problems of the American system in order to maintain the dominance of the capitalist class. It was the legitimation crisis of the capitalist state that provided the necessity to oust Nixon from office. "All of these political actors had a significant stake in limiting the scope of the crisis, defining it in certain narrow ways, and in the end, turning the crisis itself into a reaffirmation of the virtues of the American system."[8] Journalism was not the hero of Watergate but a co-conspirator in limiting its significance: "The press did its damnedest to make Nixon into the devil, so that the proper exorcism—his removal from office—could become the means of restoring faith in the system."[9]

THE CRITICAL LEFT PERSPECTIVE

The critical left also criticized the system but not from traditional or neo-Marxist perspectives. They did not see the system as a united whole serving the coherent interests of a capitalist class. Rather, they focused on the political system itself. They tried to expose the seamy side of the formalistic legal aspect of the system without relating this system to a dominating capitalist class. For the critical left, Watergate was not a sign of the systemwide crisis; rather, it was a serious violation of the very principles the system was supposed to safeguard. The spirit of the system was good but its operation was bad. The criticism focused on the dominating elite groups who operate the system. The system itself was operated in a way that contradicted its own principles and therefore greatly harmed its citizens in general. Serious violations like Watergate had become a part of "normal" politics. Watergate was only a small component of a large pattern. The system normally operationalized to repress system outsiders. But Nixon tried to further normalize the operation onto the power elite. That was the only difference between Watergate and the normal political operation of the system.

One of the most eminent critical leftists is Noam Chomsky. He asserted that the reason Nixon was subject to impeachment was not because of his evil methods against his adversaries. According to him, similar methods had been used, for years, against political radicals, but no one was punished for those illegalities and very few people even had the idea to expose those illegalities. Chomsky told people that Nixon simply made a mistake in his choice of enemies: he had on his list the chairman of IBM, senior government advisors, distinguished pundits of the press, highly placed supporters of the Democratic Party. He attacked the Washington Post, a major capitalist enterprise. And these powerful people defended themselves at once, as would be expected. Watergate? Men of power against men of power.[10]

As a leading scholar of the resource mobilization theory, William Gamson elaborated the critical left point of view in this way:

> The Nixon administration introduced an innovation of a special and limited sort: means of political combat that were normally reserved for challengers were applied to members. Nixon was able to claim, with justification, that wire-tapping, burglary, the use of agents provocateur, and the use of the Justice Department and the FBI as a weapon to harass were all practices employed by previous administrations. The special genius of the Nixon administration was to bring these techniques inside the political arena and to direct them at members, thereby causing great indignation among many who had tolerated their use against political pariahs.[11]

WHAT REALLY WORKED?—THE SOCIAL EMBEDDEDNESS OF POLITICAL INSTITUTIONS

Watergate tells us the essential things about the American political system: its character, and its operational mechanism. It reflects the substantive process of all the widely accepted major components of the formalistic authority system—election, two party system, and separation of powers, etc. First of all, it was an effort to nullify the most important national election. Secondly, parties were forced to display all their power in the process. The nature of two party politics can thus be seen quite clearly. Thirdly, all the branches of the institutionally separated powers were involved and the depth of their involvement was rarely seen under other circumstances. The nature of checks and balances thus revealed thoroughly. During the presidential impeachment process, the daily institutional routine was broken; the seemingly rationally constructed institutions could constantly be seen as irrational. Therefore, actors could be seen more clearly as socially and culturally constructed human agents rather than as structurally shaped institutional functionaries. Therefore, Watergate might be the best possible window through which to more clearly see the American political system.

In my analysis of Watergate, I touched on what Nixon and his close associates did, but I focused mainly on how the institutional system and those powerful political leaders responded to what Nixon had done. I asked less about Nixon and more about the system—How did people legitimize their action to oust a "popularly elected" President? How did they interpret the constitutional term "high crime and misdemeanor"? What forces were operating behind all of these activities? In what way did the Constitutional checks and balances work? In sum, how did the process reveal the nature of the political system—the dynamics that legitimize power into authority? To answer the questions above, I first answered the following questions: How did political actors organize? What organizational form did they adopt in order to accomplish their political goals in the Watergate affair?

For the mainstream theorists, "the system worked" means that the formal institutional systems worked and power was legitimated to become authority by its formalistic and legalistic actions for the benefit of society as a whole and for citizens as individuals. The theoretical foundation of this notion is Max Weber's classic definition on authority. Weber emphasizes formalistic and legalistic rationality about why people accept a power as authority. It implies that all different types of authority, i.e., the legitimated power, have some function and that there must be some legalistic construction based on rational reasoning for the ruled to accept the rule of certain power. But the Watergate case tells us that if we only look at the rational-legal mechanism of acceptance and overlook the social-collective dynamics of state construction, we will misplace a fundamental causal relationship.

The theoretical orientation of this book is therefore contrary to pluralist structural functionalism and neo-pluralist structural-institutionalism. Both structural-functionalism and structural-institutionalism suppose that formal state institutions are the driving forces of political processes. They assert that actors know their functional or institutional roles and they are clear about what the system or the institution can bring to them if they perform their respective institutional roles well. Therefore, their behavior will not deviate much from their positional roles and institutional duties in the system.

In this book, I regard the driving force of legitimacy as informal power dynamics, and these dynamics were more about the social formation and development of collective power dynamics than about formal state institutions. The research demonstrated that the mechanism that shaped the political process was much more than a formalistic and one-dimensional scenario. It was, rather, substantially multi-dimensional. If we solely focus on formalistic institutions and regard them as omnipresent, we might be misled and confused. In addition to the rational execution of policies and laws and the fulfillment of their institutional duties and the demand for their institutional rights and benefits, power players were socially bounded. They worked very hard for their social ties and lived in webs of interpersonal networks. They were also culturally shaped. Mental and cognitive framing and reframing in the process of power dynamics constantly shaped people's minds and hearts. The social dynamics of power included the cognitive power to rationalize, define and frame social reality; the cultural power to shape and stimulate emotional sentiment, and the interpersonal power to mobilize webs of interpersonal networks. The fixed procedural-legal rationality was much less meaningful in terms of understanding this substantial process of legitimation.

The research therefore set out to elaborate on the theory of "embeddedness."[12] It regards all political constructions as embedded in rich social relationships. The institutional structure would not work without social relations as agents. Social relations facilitated American political institutions and thus make them take root, develop, and become mature. Therefore, state institutions, like the Presidency, Congress, and the political parties, were dependent on social dynamics and were embedded in social relationships. Institutional constructions like the separation of powers and the two party system all operated through broad webs of interpersonal ties. These ties existed among inter- and intra-institutional networks and became the foundation of the Washington collective power dynamics. They went through long-term or temporary relationship formations and transformations in instances of coalition shaping and reshaping and made formal institutional power routinely embed in and work through these socially constructed webs of interpersonal ties. As Charles Peters insightfully pointed out in his book *How Washington Really Works*: "Almost everyone in government, whether he works on Capitol Hill or in the bureaucracy, is primarily concerned with his own survival. He wants to remain in Washington or in what the city symbolizes—some form of public power. Therefore from the day these people arrive in Washington they are busy building networks of people who will assure their survival in power."[13]

Therefore, besides the institutional power based on institutional positions, there was another important source of power: the informally organized and loose-knit interpersonal networks—the more people you effectively connected with in the circle of powerful politicians, the more powerful you were. The Watergate players acted just as Rollins points out: "You just really need the network, which means, in essence, that you've got to give up a little bit of your independence."[14]

DiMaggio and Louch (1998) proposed a creative notion, the "social organization of consumer market." Like them, I would regard the social dynamics in political institutions as "social organization of political institution." The formally constructed institutional "iron cage" did not always work, and when it did work, most of the time it embedded in social dynamics. It would be a great loss if someone in the area of political science overlooked the analogy between the institutional construction of government system with high level of uncertainty and the informal construction of social networks through within- and between-network dealings. Political actors' rationality could be illustrated by comparing it to economic behavior in economic organizations. DiMaggio and Louch stated about firms' choices of governance structure (contract, hierarchy, or hybrid forms) "as responses to the frequency, uncertainty, and asset specificity of transactions under conditions of bounded rationality and opportunism."[15]

Therefore, the high uncertainty routinized the significance of interpersonally and collectively constructed power dynamics in political institutions. This research views that these informal power dynamics as organized in an effective governance structure parallel to the formally constructed state institutions. Individually powerful political leaders used social dynamics in social networks in much the same way as they used formal organizations like hierarchy as alternative governance structures in their daily activities. They behaved in this way because most of their daily routine was highly uncertain and the institutional relations provided inadequate certainty and protection. Social dynamics and social contacts were effective because they embedded highly risky political activities in a relatively certain web of multiplex social relations that extend over space and time.

I therefore regard the dynamic social or collective processes as major forces that shaped and transformed the political processes. Consequently, I attribute great significance to the collective power dynamics, i.e., how people formed and maintained their power through social connections in political institutions.

The collective power dynamics were reflected by the following processes: each actor's selfish pursuit of their direct and immediate personal interests was based upon his/her calculation about the direct and immediate power relationships and his/her attempts to connect to the perceived power center; he/she thus pushed others to do the same. Those who did not make accurate calculations about their immediate power relationships and adjust their social connections accordingly would be destroyed along the way. The collective power dynamics that drive people's actions might potentially deviate from what their functional or institutional positions prescribe and thus deviate from the institutional roles they were supposed to perform. We therefore need to investigate the Washington collective power dynamics directly rather than through the lens of formal institutions.

The findings of this research points out the significance of the collective power dynamics among the webs of interpersonal ties. People were too clever to be rational; the state system was too abstract to be functional. The state system was not rationally constructed and was functionally and unmistakably serving the interests of incumbent politicians and state bureaucrats. Rather, the institutional construction of the state was embedded in the informal process of power struggle among those powerful actors. The research showed that rationally constructed state institutions, like the Presidency, Congress, the political parties, etc. were not independent and autonomous actors in the political process. Power was not institutionally separated but interpersonally shared by those powerful political leaders. Therefore, the checks and balances were embedded in the sharing of one power among those powerful politicians, not in separated many powers among the state institutions. Powerful politicians were driven by the collective power dynamics when they performed their institutional duties.

At the conclusion of this research, I regard the Washington collective power dynamics, which were based more on the informally developed webs of interpersonal networks and less on the formally and rationally constructed institutions, as the fundamental mechanism that produced the final outcome of the Watergate Affair. Here, rather than worshipping the formal institutions, I enshrine the collective-social dynamics which guaranteed the power sharing in high political circle. These social dynamics were reflected by codes and mechanisms of interpersonal networks in Washington. The former only function when they are embedded in the latter. However, this socially constructed power dynamics did not necessarily cause the state as a whole to be in an irrational or chaotic status. They might work better than the apparently rational and orderly state institutions. The formal system as a whole might be more like an unstable system with higher possibility of social control errors. However, the seemingly volatile interpersonal and collective dynamics were in fact patterned with high regularity. They were more significant than the seemingly stable formal institutions in terms of effectively stabilizing the authority system and reducing social control errors.

Therefore, the most important organizational form for us to understand in the Watergate Affair was the informal organization, i.e., the informally constructed and sustained, loose-knit interpersonal networks and collective dynamics, which existed within and across formally constructed state institutions. They were more significant than the state institutions as organizational form of actors' actions. They were structures embedded and operationalized in connections and linkages among individuals.

In the eyes of some foreigners, what happened in the Watergate affair could be attributed to unique American political institutions. However, this seemingly strange outcome was not produced by unique American political institutions. Rather, it was the universal social dynamics that played a major role. The working of the Washington collective power dynamics would highlight that the response to Nixon's offenses was "natural" and "rational". Rational people in other nation-states would "naturally" react the same to the revelations of a similar scandal as Americans did to Nixon if their political institutions were embedded in a similar set of collective power dynamics. It is the special formations and ways of development of the Washington collective power dynamics that produced some seemingly unique codes that governed the power relationships at that point in time. But, in fact, if we look deeper into the nature of this collective power dynamics, we might be able to see the universal characteristics of the American system.

The findings of this research about the Watergate Affair can thus be summarized as "the formal institutions helped" while the socially constructed and loose- knit informal power dynamics worked and finally produced the outcome. It was those informal interpersonal and collective power dynamics rather than formal state institutions which played the major role that made the system work.

THE SYSTEM WORKED, BUT FOR WHOM?—WEAPONS OF THE STRONG

What did power do to construct itself into authority? How did people in power use the socially constructed collective power dynamics to determine the overall structure of the American authority system? The answers to these questions would contradict the mainstream "system worked" and "system almost did not work" views, as well as the two left views.

American society is strong and American political institutions are effective. To understand this fact, I regard the social and culturally constructed process of legitimizing power as the core. As a new society, the United States has possessed relatively few refinements held in common. Instead, a symbolic system that many commentators have termed a "civil religion" is supposed to be what "America" is. "Democracy," "liberty," and "freedom" have become the national identity. Visitors from other lands are impressed by this national identity. At least on rational bases, Americans are supposed to internalize this symbolic system and to willingly abide by it. This is supposed to be the shared rationality. Based on it, America as a society exists and grows. In reality, the constant reiteration of those symbols has provided a common ground for the process of institutionalization of virtually all social organizations. The different social institutions in the United States of America thus meld together. Whereas American organizations and individuals within them are very practical, the ties that have been used to bind them together are very ideal and symbolic. While most people have always been concerned with their physical comfort and individual spiritual well being and most organizations have always been concerned with their practical purposes, those abstract symbols are institutionalized into each of them and therefore make America as a society stick together. However, the tension between these two features in American society constantly intensifies. How people mesh these two features together highlights the social-cultural process of legitimation.

On the macro level, these symbols are important to those in power since they stabilize the existing status quo and allow the society as a whole change in a direction that those powerful would have less motivation to resist. The ordinary citizens, too, are motivated by these symbols in their actions and dreams because their fragmented "raw" interests and desires and wants are shaped and framed by these symbols. And more importantly, the effective governance of these symbols over the political activities of those in power is deeply rooted in the micro patterns of interpersonal interactions. A clear example is that the sharing of power is essential to making the institutional construction flexible, responding, and accommodating.

In the case of Watergate, it was especially important to invoke the symbolic system to unite the people in power though the collective power dynamics. At the same time, the symbolic system served as a means to convince the ordinary citizens about the fairness of the system without their direct participation. Since Watergate was not a conflict over a particular policy or a specific piece of legislation, it could be used to shape citizens' habits of heart. Individual self-interest and normal political loyalties would be connected to fundamental beliefs and deep-rooted and "lofty" sentiments. These beliefs and emotions could be induced less from the "facts" than from the symbolic meanings of those facts. For those in power who strove to unify themselves in a power struggle and to stabilize the political system along the way, Watergate would become a symbolic issue in the socially constructed power dynamics.

Therefore, powerful political leaders first needed to work out among themselves the rationale and mental frame of their governance. They were also in need and capable of educating ordinary people about what was important to them. To all the ordinary citizens, this frame was important and had the power to reshape their minds and hearts. That is to say, while what their daily "raw" thinking and wanting were not necessarily important to themselves, what political leaders were trying to work out was truly important to everybody. In this way, the socially and culturally constructed power dynamics would legitimize power into authority by imposing an image "WE are fighting for YOU". Here, both the "we" and the "you" were transformed by the power dynamics. The idea was clear: the power struggle among those powerful political leaders was a healthy process. It would work out the differences among those powerful and guarantee a power-sharing status quo. The behavior codes of power sharing and compromise in the high political circles were also important to the society as a whole. It was in this way that the power struggle over Watergate among powerful political leaders worked for citizens in general.

The reality that this idea was trying to reflect was also clear: the Washington collective power dynamics worked powerfully behind all of this. The representative political system only worked through collective power dynamics; powerful politicians represented ordinary people only after they effectively worked things out among themselves and effectively educated citizenry. One feature that could best reflect the nature of authority here was that authority was more about the effectively mobilized social power and less about, as Weber asserted, the legal power.

Here we can see clearly that the common assumption on the authority system is wrong. A rational authority is supposed to be based on representing the interests of those who are supposed to accept power as authority. However, Watergate tells us that all of these interests were socially constructed before they were represented. There was no such a thing as "raw" interest of the citizenry without it being crafted. In the Watergate case, all interests were reframed before they became the public agenda. All others, as they were reflected by the public opinion polls, were chaotic, self-contradictory, and ever-changing. This might not be necessarily true, but it was true for the people who were powerful enough to actively participate in the process of social construction. It was a political truth with practical function. The function of the collective power dynamics would be to frame and shape the chaotic and unstable public interests and to make them stable and reasonable. Because the powerful political leaders had the power to frame and shape those interests, they inevitably and naturally became the strong compared to ordinary citizens and, therefore, the agenda-setting, event-framing clearly displayed "weapons of the strong."

In sum, this research revealed a social and cultural process that showed the strength and flexibility of the American political system. This process was driven by socially constructed power dynamics. The book has also developed an understanding about the linkage on macro and micro levels of the political process. It is reflected by the macro social-cultural construction of events through the micro socially constructed power dynamics. Authority as it was reflected by the Watergate Affair could be regarded as the reflection of a process in which the power structure was based on the informal and socially constructed power dynamics. It was the most socially connected people that constantly moved the collective power dynamics in search of legitimacy for the dominance of their networks in a formalistic sense. The enshrined formalistic and institutionalized authority system was therefore not so rational, orderly, and functional. The strength of the American authority system was more reflected by the culturally and socially constructed power dynamics.

However, while the socially constructed power dynamics could effectively put a serious violation like Watergate to a timely end and stabilize the system, it also had down side. The same "sacred" collective power dynamics also insulated and isolated the political leaders in Washington. It made the connection between the powerful and the powerless less organic and more artificial. They became "weapons of the strong." When these "weapons" were used by the strong for their dominance, they facilitated two fundamental problems in the American political system. The first one was the insulation of the high circle of power from the rest of society; the second was the fragmentation of the society in which the entire political process takes place. Concretely speaking, it effectively insulates the system from citizens who could not in any way establish linkages, or paths, to the powerful webs of interpersonal ties. And this kind of political construction and the organization of political leaders also furthered the fragmentation of the society as a whole.

According to pluralist view, any social group can gain access to the system as long as they play by the institutionalized rules. But as Gamson made clear: "The pluralist image, then, is a half-truth."[16] "It is a members-only system with formidable ways of keeping the door shut."[17] Gamson supports his assertion by demonstrating that the institutionalized formal state power shut the door for ordinary citizens.

This research supports Gamson's assertion but from another angle. It was the Washington collective power dynamics that made it possible that only those insiders who were capable of weaving or penetrating into those powerful social webs could gain access to the political process. Since these power dynamics are socially constructed, the social force is very strong in terms of selectively accepting insiders who are socially and culturally acceptable to the circles of significant others; outsiders without proper social connections would be naturally insulated from those socially constructed power dynamics. For outsiders, the barrier of social networking is formidable because the socially constructed power dynamics are subtle — it is very hard for outsiders to find regularity in them. For them, nothing is fixed. But for insiders, everything is subtle but clear and firm. It would not be difficult, in a subtle way by following those socially constructed "secret" and "sacred" codes only masterable by insiders, to apply different rules to insiders and outsiders in terms of acceptability to the powerful interpersonal webs. In this subtle way, outsiders are naturally prevented from gaining access to the system. This is the informal, besides the formal, way the "pluralist" system works — it would naturally provide a role to play in the power dynamics to insider-established groups while insulating the system from any outsider-challengers. It is thus the most effective measure to deal with "tough" outside challengers who might upset the system and cause instability.

In this situation, the legally and institutionally constructed "open field" for political competition and voluntary participation is thus not necessarily the case. The collective power dynamics have made politics "insiders only." Even insiders might be divided hierarchically according to their social connections to the power center. The political system embedded in this type of social construction might be strong, stable, and powerful, but it is by no means equal for every citizen. Lack of equal access to power would be the most serious weakness of the system because it would insulate the power center and fragment the society. It thus produces limitation in terms of effectively exercising the state authority over citizens in general.

TOWARD A NEO-PROGRESSIVISM

I agree with the conservative view that the end result of the Watergate Affair reflected the strength of American political system; but I don't think the system worked as it was. I share the concern with the liberal view about the uncertainty of the formal state institutions; but I don't think we can fix the system by adding more laws and government agencies. Similar to the leftist view, I believe Watergate was a social construction driven by power dynamics; but I don't think Watergate was an unregulated power game in which the only nature was men of power against men of power. I also think it would not be fair and realistic to denounce the entire system simply because of its flexibility and sensitivity to the existing power dynamics.

My conclusion is that the Washington collective power dynamics worked for the powerful political leaders in Washington and, to a lesser degree, for the society as a whole. This was because the formalized institutional system worked only in the sense that it successfully accommodated and facilitated the socially embedded collective power dynamics. This flexibility was reflected by the timely response of the former to the latter. The formal system did not rigidly suppress the socially grown power. On the contrary, it quickly responded to the ever-changing socially constructed power dynamics among power players. More importantly, the socially constructed power dynamics are patterned with high regularity. They have been playing a crucial role in making the formal system stable, powerful, and healthy. The beauty of the American political system as it was reflected by this research was the fact that it guaranteed power sharing. This was the foundation to make the political system in particular, and society in general, better. Therefore, the way to make the formal system work better with more certainty would be to make it more flexible to the informal social relationships. Furthermore, the collective power dynamics might be able to shape political leaders and make them work together to benefit the country as a whole. However, to make this happen, to make the society stronger and the system more effective, a precondition would be progressively constructing healthy social dynamics that would go beyond the Washington beltway. We need the healthy national collective power dynamics in addition to the Washington collective power. The former must be able to control the latter. This is the key point this book is trying to address.

Both Putnam and Skocpol proposed similar views. They highlighted the significance of community construction and development on the civic side of the political system.[18] However, they did not reveal the deep-seated social dynamics inside the state institutional construction. They overlooked the issue of the social embeddedness of political institutions. Therefore their research would not be able to reflect the social process of power construction and power dynamics in the state system as a whole. Based upon the research presented in this book, I would regard Granovetter's model, the strength of weak ties, as a better theoretical framework.

As the research in this book demonstrates, collective power dynamics play a significant role in the political process, but these dynamics are limited in terms of bridging Washington and the nation. Therefore, the American state institutions are embedded in limited social dynamics which would confine the system to Washington high circles only. The formal state institutions are not capable of effectively connecting the entire nation because they are superficial and ineffective. Whereas we cannot rely on formal state institutions to accomplish all our political goals, we need a national collective power to genuinely connect the nation as an organic whole. Lack of weak ties between the powerful and the less powerful might be the major problem that inhibits the genuine connection of the nation and harms the cohesiveness of the political process. It is thus a major cause of societal fragmentation. According to Granovetter,

> "people rarely act on mass-media information unless it is also transmitted through personal ties; otherwise one has no particular reason to think that an advertised product or an organization should be taken seriously." "Trust in leaders is integrally related to the capacity to predict and affect their behavior. Leaders, for their part, have little motivation to be responsive or even trustworthy toward those to whom they have no direct or indirect connection. Thus, network fragmentation, by reducing drastically the number of paths from any leader to his potential followers, would inhibit trust in such leaders. This inhibition, furthermore, would not be entirely irrational."[19]

Also, according to Granovetter, a sign of powerlessness is a lack of weak ties as resources at their disposal. This is especially true among working class people because of their simple work and lifestyles and their closer involvement in few strong ties.

Therefore, the strong tie—weak tie approach might enable us to find the source of the strength of a political system. It might help us to answer: How could the system involve more and more ordinary citizens into its process but at the same time guarantee its stability and healthy operation? How could a genuine connection be built up between powerful politicians and outsiders? For those excluded from the process of the system, how could we help them develop the weak ties if the lack of weak ties constitutes the major hurdle to them gaining access to the authority system? How could we clearly utilize all the subtle but powerful social dynamics to facilitate the genuine connection in the authority system? The key point here is that, for a society in general and for a political system in particular, the more weak ties among different kinds of people, especially between the people with power and the people without much power, the better. The key issue is to institutionalize more channels and paths that would facilitate and nourish the development and growth of more and more weak ties among citizens in the political process.

I would like to label this approach neo-progressivism.

NOTES

1. Lipset, S.M. and E. Raab. "An Appointment with Watergate" *Commentary* 36 (Sept. 1973): 37.

2. Lipset and Raab. "An Appointment with Watergate", 42-43.

3. Huntington, Samuel F. "The Democratic Distemper" *The Public Interest* 39 (Spring 1975): 10.

4. Mintz, Morton and Jerry S. Cohen. *Power Inc.: public and private rulers and how to make them accountable.* (New York: The Viking Press, 1976), xxvi.

5. Mintz and Cohen. *Power Inc.,* xxvii

6. Mintz and Cohen. *Power Inc.,* 19.

7. Mintz and Cohen. *Power Inc.,* 23.

8. San Francisco Bay Area Kapitalistate Group, "Watergate, or the Eighteenth Brumaire of Richard Nixon" *Kapitalistate* No.3 (Spring 1975), 15.

9. San Francisco Bay Area Kapitalistate Group "Watergate, or the Eighteenth Brumaire of Richard Nixon", 18.

10 Chomsky, Noam. "Watergate: A Skeptical View" *New York Review of Books* 20 (September 1973), 8.

11. Gamson, William. *The Strategy of Social Protest* 2nd ed. (Belmont, CA: Wadsworth Publishing Company—A Division of Wadsworth, Inc., 1990), 142.

12. Granovetter, Mark. "The Strength of Weak Ties" *American Journal of Sociology* 78, no.6 (1972): 1360-1380; "Economic Action and Social Structure: the problem of embeddedness" *American Journal of Sociology* 91, no.3 (1985): 481-510.

13. Peters, Charles. *How Washington Really Works.* (Reading, MA: Addison-Wesley Publishing Co., 1980), 5-6.

14. Smith, Hedrick. *The Power Game—how Washington works*. (New York: Random House, 1988), 98-99.

15. DiMaggio, Paul and Hugh Louch. "Social Embedded Consumer Transactions: for what kinds of purchases do people most often use networks?" *American Sociological Review* 63 (October 1998): 619-637.

16. Gamson, William. *The Strategy of Social Protest* 2nd ed. (Belmont, CA: Wadsworth Publishing Company—A Division of Wadsworth, Inc., 1990), 142.

17. Gamson, *The Strategy of Social Protest,* 177.

18. Putnam, Robert D. *Bowling Alone: the collapse and revival of American community* (New York: Simon and Schuster, 2000); Skocpol, Theda. *Diminished Democracy: from membership to management in American civil life.* (Norman: University of Oklahoma Press, 2003)

19. Granovetter, "The Strength of Weak Ties", 1374.

Appendix

Discussion on Methodology

QUALITATIVE METHOD IN GENERAL

Why do I choose a qualitative method over a quantitative one? My epistemological consideration is that sociology differs from Western European style natural sciences, which base their methodology on metaphysics. Natural sciences therefore cut nature into pieces, focus on only few variables, and find the relationships between them. They do not have to be concerned about the organic interconnections between all the possible variables, and treat the entire universe as an organic whole. It is because of this that they are in an advantageous position to make research easier to handle, more reliable, and more likely to achieve theoretical validity.

Sociology, however, originally tries to understand the society as an organic whole through studies of the interconnected relationships in society. Its productivity is low; it creates more ambiguities than it provides clear answers. Therefore, survey research, together with experimental research and all other quantitative research strategies, tries to break away from this "old fashioned, unscientific way" of studying society. These quantitative methods, trying to imitate natural sciences, cut society into variables on the structured questionnaire or conduct standardized experimental procedures. So far, they have achieved great progress for the study of society. It is clear that these approaches are very important to construct tightly articulated hypotheses; also, it is not too difficult to apply it to the circumstances where a researcher can isolate social phenomena freely without too much hurting their original character and composition. However, this kind of methodology easily produces one-sided results. And, more importantly, it is difficult for quantitative research to achieve the same level of progress as natural sciences do. The reason lies in the nature of its research object—the society. It is because social phenomena are so interrelated and it would be too difficult to isolate a social phenomenon without distorting its original nature. Society is, in its nature, an organic whole with countless interrelated variables moving in and around it. It does not allow any human action upon it to overlook this fact by cutting it into pieces for the sake of research. Society is not so easily manipulated as nature. It often fiercely resists the "divide and rule" strategy. Unlike nature, which only takes revenge in a passive way, society actively resists human action based upon the "fragmentary and piecemeal understanding" of it.

Due to the inseparable interconnectedness of society, it might be more reasonable for sociological research to adopt the "natural" way of doing research. These ways include grounding theory in social reality by using comparative and historical study and grand theory-oriented research. It's very important to cover as much social phenomena as possible without cutting them off too hard from their originally connected organic whole. For achieving a high degree of theoretical understanding about society, it might be more productive to treat society this way. This kind of research practice has thus gained ground in sociology through its unique way of grasping interconnected social relationships rather than separated variables. For better understanding the Watergate affair, it might also be better to adopt a qualitative method in order to make sense of the case in a systematic, coherent way and treat the case as an interconnected organic whole.

THEORY ELABORATION METHODOLOGY

The theory elaboration approach[1] is a qualitative methodology. The task of elaboration is accomplished through case studies in which theory is interplayed with the entirety of the case. A central feature of this analytic approach is its reliance on the story line, or plot, as its grounding for theory verification and falsification. It does not use the grounded theory type of constant comparative analysis. For this method, theory may not be generated initially from the data; but, if the existing mature theory gets affiliated with the complete and coherent story line of the case development, it will be verified, falsified, modified, and developed at the same time as it is meticulously played against the unique case.

The major difference between this method and other approaches of qualitative research is its emphasis upon theory verification and theory development at the same time. It therefore explicitly involves verifying a theory and generating new aspects of this theory as two inseparable parts of the same process. Researcher can focus on various levels of the existing mature theory by shifting unit of analysis, i.e., organizational level and social forms. Theory elaboration method can be best directed at elaborating substantive theories rather than elaborating formal theories.

I found that the theory elaboration method can better reflect the internal logic of scientific development. From old Hebrew biblical teachings to ancient Chinese Confucianism, and all the way to Kant, many great thinkers of the past believed the limitation of human knowledgeability and that the universe, our society included, is beyond our human to comprehend in a total and systematic way. However, modern science provided an antithesis, and filled us with full confidence of discovering the laws of the universe by accumulating knowledge piece by piece. Each tested and proven scientific knowledge is final in terms of our understanding of that specific piece of the universe. If we put all the pieces together, step by step, we would be able to solve the puzzle and know the universe as a whole. Karl Popper[2] and Thomas Kuhn[3] proposed a synthesis. Popper asserted that scientific discovery can only falsify, rather than prove, a theory. Scientific development is a process of falsification. In this way, the boundary of each theory can be clearer and clearer. Human knowledgeability is reflected this way; i.e., it is not reflected by the accumulation of proven scientific discoveries as building blocks. Kuhn's thought of "paradigm" made the human subjective factor clearer in seemingly pure objective scientific research. We are all in a box that we cannot see. Scientific development is, most of the time, a process of quantitatively accumulating knowledge in one box. It is only occasionally that people jump into another box and start developing qualitatively different knowledge in that box.

Vaughan's methodology is in accordance with the synthesis by Popper and Kuhn. The key point of her methodology is the shifting unit of analysis.

First, we are able to falsify a theory by moving it to another social form or another organizational level. Regular qualitative methodology, like the widely used grounded theory, tries to either prove an existing theory or, more often, to develop new theory. It cannot do both at the same time. This is the typical modern scientific way of thinking. By shifting the unit of analysis, the theory elaboration methodology is able to make researchers verify and falsify a theory and discover new facts at the same time. In the theory elaboration process, no theory is proved as a final product; but the boundary of each theory becomes clearer and clearer. Previous research can thus be bridged to current research; at the same time, an avenue is therefore open for future research; new theory based on old one can be developed.

Second, it is possible to avoid unnecessary repetition in terms of empirical research on one theory in a certain paradigm box. It is certain that it is not easy to break through a paradigm. But regular research methodology can only encourage researches to close themselves in a box without even seeing it. It is very common that we do many, many empirical studies and end up with results only repeating a theory without improving the depth and scope of this theory. This is the typical phenomenon, as Kuhn pointed out, of "closed and boxed" research. Although theory elaboration methodology cannot guarantee paradigm shifts (no methodology has such a magic wand), it opens a much wider avenue and provides a much greater potentiality for a research to jump into another paradigm with qualitatively elaborated theory as the stepping stone.

In summary, this methodology gives me clear rules to follow and at the same time gives me enough space to fit in. As a theory-oriented project, this work attempts to target a fundamental theoretical issue. As many theory-oriented researches that have benefited from the theory elaboration methodology, this research shifts the unit of analysis of the theory of social embeddedness from typical social arena to state authority. It therefore opens up this theory to embrace broader fields rather than closing it in a confined area.

ISSUES OF VALIDITY AND RELIABILITY

The two major components of a scientific research design are its reliability and its validity. It is through reliability that science achieves its objectivity; it is through validity that science achieves its logical soundness and theoretical integrity. I have no doubt that both reliability and validity are very important for any research and I have determined to make every effort to achieve them at as high a level as possible in my research. But, I could not have done this without the guidance of the theory elaboration methodology.

A scientific goal requires that, when we construct our research project and proceed with it, we should always be aware of the relevance of each of our measures to our theoretical scheme, that is, we should aim to achieve high level of internal validity. Theory elaboration method makes this task easier. Unlike survey research, which has very rigid categories and standardized operating procedures, theory elaboration sets out from an existing mature theory and provides a relative flexibility in terms of constructing categories and operating within them. In this sense, a research project using theory elaboration method is more likely to achieve a higher level logical soundness and theoretical integrity than any quantitative research. Based upon its advantage in terms of internal validity, theory elaboration method facilitates in research a distinctive virtue in terms of theory generation and construction.

In terms of reliability, we, as researchers who are making every effort to convince others in both scientist community and outside of it, should make our research as consistent as possible and our research results generalizeable in other cases. Anyone who replicates our research should be able to achieve the same result. Also, the research results should be applicable when they are used to analyze other social organizations in other situations. This should be one of our goals when we start designing our project. But the situation in real research is not so ideal. It is much more complicated for historical research to achieve as high a scientific standard as any quantitative research. Two issues threaten the scientific standard in my research. One of the threats is that my research has representative problem and is not so scientifically generalizable as quantitative research. However, the more threatening issue is reliability. It is certain that quantitative research like survey research is also highly subjective in terms of questionnaire construction, which includes as much bias as historical data collection does. However, its operational procedures and data analyses are much more standardized and much less subjective than those of historical research.

Although it is difficult to achieve as high a reliability as in quantitative research, it is not totally impossible for us to approach reliability by using the theory elaboration method. The concrete way is that we should focus on the natural story line with "hard" facts as its building blocks. Anybody who gets in touch with the data would be able to discover the same facts. Anybody who wants to verify our research report can examine the same data and should be able to find the same story line. As long as they follow the story-line we present, they should reach the same conclusion based upon those facts. Also, because of the shifting units of analysis, the scope and space of applicability of the elaborated theory is expanded. It will be more generalizable to a broader sphere with more cases included. By comparison to other cases, the generalizability of the elaborated theory is in an ever-expanding process. Therefore, the reliability of the research using theory elaboration methodology is solidly embedded in the case comparison and scope expansion.

In this way, the theory elaboration method makes both of the threatening issues above only hurt the face value of the scientific nature of a historical research. Historical research can thus maintain a rigorous scientific exploration without being embarrassed by its seemingly lower level of generalizability and reliability. During many years of practice and methodological construction, theory elaboration method has developed a complete set of principles and techniques, which can, to a large extent, overcome the generalizability and reliability problem. Certain general procedures have made this method effective and influential. Three special issues are addressed as follows.

THE STORY-LINE STRATEGY

For conducting research based on an established theory without losing rigorous validity and reliability, a key issue is how to deal with the relationship between theory and data. Should I use theory as a guide to lead us into empirical exploration or should I leave existing theory aside and only allow theory to emerge from data? There are two major approaches beside the theory elaboration methodology. The first is the "testing" approach, i.e., theory as a group of hypotheses and data are collected to test these hypotheses in a qualitative or quantitative way. It requires forcibly cutting data into pieces from organically interconnected social reality. If researchers are not careful enough to strictly stick to every variable to their problem, they are very easy to commit the mistake of forcing fit. Therefore, it has high potentiality of improper validity. The second is the traditional approach of historical research, i.e., theory can only be allowed to emerge from data. Because data only reflect the concrete context and this context may very well theoretically differ from other context, it is hard to generalize theory properly. Its generalizability is greatly limited. Therefore, theory produced from historical methodology has a high potentiality of improper reliability.

A major procedure proposed by the theory elaboration methodology is the systematic, coherent "story-line" requirement. The existing theory would thus be verified and new aspects of it would be generated through the construction of a complete and coherent story-line. Researchers using this method would be able to ask themselves after they constructed the story-line for the case: How has the existing theory interplayed with the case in its entirety and how have new aspects of this theory emerged from this interplay? How has a story-line showed the close correspondence between theoretical concepts and data? How has every concept and argument of this existing theory been grounded in the story-line?

I did not use the grounded theory type of constant comparison to achieve parsimony of variables and formulation. I started my research with a well established theory and a clear theoretical framework. It would have been very easy for me to be pre-occupied by the existing theoretical framework. This would have created a problem of forcing fit, which would hurt the validity of this research. I would have been in great danger of losing scientific rigor. The reason was that, once I started, my research would have naturally been on an irreversible track of "theoretical sampling." My focus would have been driven by the efforts of closing theoretical gaps by selectively collecting data under the direction of my pre-existing theoretical framework. For typical research using grounded theory method, this procedure is acceptable. According to the masters of grounded theory Glaser and Strauss: "Theoretical sampling is the process of data collection for generating theory whereby the analyst jointly collects, codes, and analyzes his data and decides what data to collect next and where to find them, in order to develop his theory as it emerges. This process of data collection is controlled by the emerging theory, whether substantive or formal."[4]

However, this would not be the step I was supposed to take because of the requirements of the theory elaboration method. Theory elaboration methodology allows a research to start with an established theory, but it is data that dictate the entire elaboration process. Theory can only be elaborated through discovery. The discovery process occurs through the systematic use of cases. In order not to be pre-occupied by pre-existing theoretical orientation and to guarantee the scientific rigor, the strategy requires research to explain as fully as possible its plot. Each case is treated as a unique and interconnected whole without any violation to its internal integrity. The relationship between all parts and the whole must be clearly explained and parts cannot be treated as evidence without taking the whole into account. The task of elaboration can only be accomplished through constructing a complete story-line for the case.

In order to keep a close correspondence of theory and data in a situation where I tried to expand the scope of the applicability of the theory to a wider range, I focused on the story-line of the Watergate case in its entirety. Instead of sampling data based on a theoretical framework, I set out to construct a complete, coherent plot of the case against my theoretical statements. The uniqueness and the idiosyncratic details of the case thus got the most attention. It drew my description and narrative away from my pre-existing theoretical framework and forced me to focus on the plot of the story development. I tried, during constructing the story-line of the case, to mentally separate my pre-existing theoretical framework from the natural plot of the case. I also tried to mention it as little as possible, unless it helped the story-line. In the more than two-hundred-page story constructions, I did not mention much about my pre-existing theoretical framework. In this way, I avoided cutting interconnected cases into pieces and isolating a portion of them to force a fit to the theory. In this way, by keeping the integrity and uniqueness of the Watergate case, i.e., its own "story-line," I elaborated the theory of social embeddedness without having to fear the "forcing fit" problem. The problems of validity and reliability on this front were thus minimized.

SENSITIZING CONCEPTS

By adhering to grounding the theory in data, the concepts in this book manifest two essential features proposed by Glaser and Strauss, which were also consistent with the essential logic of the theory elaboration approach: "First, the concepts should be analytic—sufficiently generalized to designate characteristics of concrete entities, not the entities themselves. They should also be sensitizing—yield a 'meaningful' picture, abetted by apt illustrations that enable one to grasp the reference in terms of one's own experience."[5] To guarantee a high level of reliability, I used as many definitive concepts as possible. I tried to preserve, as much as possible, the sharp analytical feature of these concepts that could be used analytically to many other circumstances and other types of organizations, and, thus, become the fundamental bricks of formal theories about human organizations in general. At the same time, many of my concepts were very sensitizing. This research, to a large extent, departed from loosely constructed sensitizing concepts, which were much more closely situated in a concrete context, rather than in the formalized propositions and hypotheses. Unlike the definitive concepts, these sensitizing concepts suggested a direction around which to look, not what to see.[6] The sensitizing concepts are vague but powerful in terms of directing me in certain directions to look for what I should see. Setting out from these concepts enabled me to establish a system of concepts, which included both definitive concepts and sensitizing ones. For those definitive ones, I tried to make them directly and clearly correspondent to certain social groups of people and certain social facts in reality. Readers can see these people or these phenomena in their daily lives rather than just feel them or sense them. For instance, instead of using "men of power," I used "political leaders" or "powerful politicians"; instead of using "public" "people", I used organized or unorganized citizens. For some sensitizing concepts, I embedded them in concrete historical contexts and provided rich examples to illustrate their basic properties. I tried to draw impressionist pictures of them. It was like illustrating a fast running horse with a vague image but clear sensation. Although I did not specify the weight, the height, the color, and other features of the horse, I conveyed a message and feeling about a powerful horse. My readers therefore know where to look for a horse like this. For instance, the concept "Washington collective power dynamics" is a sensitizing one. Based upon such a conceptualization, the lack of reliability problem caused by the sensitizing concepts and the lack of validity problem caused by the definitive concepts were minimized.

SECONDARY DATA

It was clear to me that I was not able to do research of this sort other than using secondary data. There are many advantages of using secondary data. First of all, I thus touched upon broad issues across time and space. Secondly, I got data on the issues that interviewees would never have wanted to talk about and field observers would never get a chance to see. Furthermore, what I saw were the actual actions of those actors and the consequences of those actions as they actually happened and were recorded in history. Also, the research benefited from ever increasingly accumulated and documented historical records. With historical distance, much secondary data further provided a more accurate account about what really happened that contemporaries would not have been able to see. Secondary analyses, the more polished form of secondary data, not only made the richer and broader data available, but also provided valuable broad comparisons that no other research approach could offer.

However, the conventional methodologies, both the quantitative hypothesis testing method and qualitative grounded theory, naturally require researchers to gather first hand data because (1) for the former, it is important to discover new data in order to test the concepts and subconcepts of each hypothesis in order to achieve validity and generalizability. Secondary data would not be adequate at all; (2) for the latter, it is necessary to discover new facts in order to let new theory emerge. Even in the case of verification, grounded theory requires first hand data.

The theory elaboration methodology enabled me to gather evidence for this study from synthesized secondary sources, like the published historical and journalistic studies and memoirs. Contrary to other methodologies, it actually encourages researchers to use this kind of data because they can be used as a bias-reduction strategy. Secondary analyses, especially those well-developed through historical research, would not readily fit our theoretical presumptions. They are more difficult to manipulate than the first hand data, and therefore minimize the problem of "forcing fit."

But, still, there are many disadvantages of using secondary data and secondary analyses. First of all, naturally, secondary data tend to include much more dramatic events than those ordinary ones because dramatic occurrences usually tend to be best remembered and recorded. But sometimes the ordinary ones are more important in terms of understanding the development of the case. Facing a set of such obviously skewed data, the "story-line" approach helped me set a proper frame of internal logic. I followed the internal logic and natural "story line" rather than the availability of data.

Another problem for secondary data and secondary analyses is that they tend to mix hard facts with soft opinions. The story-line strategy also provided a remedy for this. It forced me to focus on hard facts rather than on soft opinions since only the hard facts could be the building blocks of a complete plot. To better follow the "story-line," I focused on "facts" rather than on "opinions". The latter was used as data only when it had the value of demonstrating an actor's mentality in an unfolding event.

I did some textual research but did not present those collateral data, in order to keep a clear story line and make my text easier for readers to follow and less confusing. In this way, I avoided putting myself and my readers through the swamp of textual criticism. Certainly, there was a trade-off. I did not introduce a variety of sources to show whether there were some controversies about certain historical facts or whether everyone was saying the same thing about certain historical facts. I therefore faced the task of making my secondary data more reliable. I tried to meet two critical standards in selecting these data: first, all of my data should be widely publicized and much discussed. All data I used were not hearsay; they were all publicly known as true or were proven true by later history. Secondly, in cases where there were controversies in terms of historical facts, I followed the most authoritative one and did not pick up many different accounts. But I marked the multiple sources in different accounts in those important historical junctures in order for readers to have a relatively clear road-map to trace the details of those facts in my description and narrative. In these ways, the secondary data strategy helped rather than hurt the quality of the research and enhanced its level of reliability and validity.

OPEN-ENDED RESEARCH

The data constraint very much limited my exploration. Also, the subjective nature of historical research makes the understanding of the meaning of each piece of data dependant, to a large extent, on the ever-developing subjective interpretations of historical facts. It is also influenced by the intersubjective construction of meanings in history. This situation forces me into the position of still having many questions without answers at the end of my research. As a result, although I strove to perform research that can achieve greater specificity, I might have created "greater ambiguity".

Fortunately, the theory elaboration methodology allows this project to be an open-ended one. At a time when it would not be objectively realistic to give final answers to all theoretical questions raised by this research, this methodology also makes it not subjectively desirable to do so. This methodological flexibility is especially important to this project. The ambiguous results of this research thus become both disappointing and promising. The illustrations of the intricate details of this case have brought forward many loose ends in the eyes of other researchers. From the perspective of theory elaboration, this result can possibly push us toward future theoretical breakthroughs. Additional questions would be asked in the future and to answer these questions, the theory of a neo-progressivism would be further specified and developed.

NOTES

1. Vaughan, Diane. "Theory Elaboration: the heuristics of case analysis" in *What is a Case? issues in the logic of social inquiry.* Charles C. Ragin and Haward S. Becker, eds. New York: Cambridge University Press, 1992.

2. Popper, Karl R. *The Logic of Scientific Discovery*. London: Hutchinson Publisher, 1968

3. Kuhn, Thomas S. *The Structure of Scientific Revolution* (2nd ed., enlarged). Chicago: University of Chicago Press, 1970.

4. Glaser, Barney G. and Anselm L. Strauss. *The Discovery of Grounded Theory: strategies for qualitative research*. (New York: Aldine De Gruyter, 1967), 45.

5. Glaser, Barney G. and Anselm L. Strauss. *The Discovery of Grounded Theory*, 38–39.

6. Blumer, Herbert. "What is Wrong with Social Theory", *American Sociological Review*, 19 (1953): 3–10.

Bibliography

Ben-Veniste, Richard and George Frampton Jr. *Stonewall: The Real Story of the Watergate Prosecution.* New York: Simon & Schuster, 1977.

Bernstein, Berton J. "The Road to Watergate and Beyond: the Growth and Abuse of Executive Authority since 1940." *Law and Contemporary Problems* 40, no. 84 (1976).

Bernstein, Carl and Bob Woodward. *All the President's Men.* New York: Simon & Schuster, 1974.

Bickel, Alexander. "Watergate and the Legal Order" *Commentary* 57 (January 1974): 19–24.

Blumer, Herbert. "What is Wrong with Social Theory" *American Sociological Review,* 19 (1953): 3–10.

Bourdieu, Pierre, and Jean-Claude Passeron. *Reproduction in Education, Society, and Culture.* Trans. Richard Nice and Tom Bottommore. London: Sage, 1977.

Bourjaily, Vance. "The Triumph of Watergate: the Final Act" *American Heritage* 35 (1980): 32.

Chester, Lewis, Cal McCrystal, Stephen Aris, and William Shawcross. *Watergate: The Full Inside Story.* New York: Random House, 1978.

Chomsky, Noam. "Watergate: A Skeptical View" *New York Review of Books* 20 (September 1973).

Cole, Richard and David Caputo, "Presidential Control of the Senior Civil Service," *American Political Review* 73 (June 1979).

Congressional Quarterly Inc. *Watergate: Chronology of a Crisis* Washington D.C.: Congressional Quarterly Press, 1975.

Crawford, Alan. *Thunder on Right: The "New Right" and the Politics of Resentment.* New York: Pantheon, 1980.

Dahl, Robert A. *Who Governs? Democracy and Power in an American City.* New Heaven, CT.: Yale University Press, 1961.

———. *Pluralist Democracy in the United States* Chicago: Rand McNally, 1967.

Dash, Samuel. *Chief Counsel: Inside the Ervin Committee.* New York: Random House, 1976.
Davidson, Roger H. and Walter J. Oleszek. *Congress and Its Members.* 7th ed. Washington, D.C.: CQ Press, 2000.
Dean, John W. III. *Blind Ambition: The White House Years.* New York: Simon & Shuster, 1976.
DiMaggio, Paul and Hugh Louch. "Social Embedded Consumer Transactions: for what kinds of purchases do people most often use networks?" *American Sociological Review* 63 (October 1998): 619–637.
Dobrovir, William A. Joseph D. Gebhardt, Samuel J. Buffone, and Andra H. Oakes. *The Offenses of Nixon: A Guide for the People of the United States.* New York: The New York Times Book Co., 1973.
Donner, Frank J. *The Age of Surveillance.* New York: Knoff, 1980.
Doyle, James. *Not Above the Law: The Battle of Watergate Prosecutors Cox and Jaworski.* New York: William Morrow, 1977.
Drew, Elizabeth. *Washington Journal: the events of 1973–1974.* New York: Random House, 1975.
Edwards, Lee. *Goldwater—the man who made a revolution.* Washington D.C.: Regnery Publishing, Inc.—an Eagle Publishing Co, D.C., 1995.
Ehrlichman, John. *Witness to Power: The Nixon Years.* New York: Simon & Schuster, 1982.
Ervin, Sam Jr. *The Whole Truth: The Watergate Conspiracy.* New York: Random House, 1980.
Evens, Rowland and Robert Novak. *Nixon in the White House: The Frustration of Power.* New York: Random House, 1971.
Fenno, Richard Jr. *Home Style: House Members in Their Districts.* Boston: Little, Brown, 1978.
Field, Jack New. *A Prophetic Minority.* New York: New American Library, 1966.
Fiorina, Morris. *Congress: Keystone of the Washington Establishment.* 2nd ed. New Haven, CT.; Yale University Press, 1989.
Friedman, Leon and William F. Levantrosser (eds.) *Watergate and Afterward—the legacy of Richard M. Nixon.* Westport, Connecticut & London: Greenwood Press, 1992.
Gamson, William. *The Strategy of Social Protest* 2nd ed. Belmont, CA: Wadsworth Publishing Company—A Division of Wadsworth, Inc., 1990.
Gardner, J. "The Colonies Will Overcome" *The New York Times*, May 16, 1973.
Glaser, Barney G. and Anselm L. Strauss. *The Discovery of Grounded Theory: strategies for qualitative research.* New York: Aldine De Gruyter, 1967.
Goldberg, Robert Alan. *Barry Goldwater.* New Haven, CT.: Yale University Press, 1995.
Goldwater, Barry M. *With No Apologies—the personal and political memoirs of United States Senator Barry M. Goldwater.* New York: William Morrow, 1979.
Goldwater, Barry M. and Jack Casserly. *Goldwater.* New York: Doubleday, 1988.
Granovetter, Mark. "The Strength of Weak Ties" *American Journal of Sociology* 78, no. 6 (1972): 1360–1380.

———. "Economic Action and Social Structure: the problem of embeddedness" *American Journal of Sociology* 91, no.3 (1985): 481–510.

Halberstam, David. *The Powers That Be.* New York: Knopf, 1979.

Haldeman, H.R.and Joseph DiMona. *The End of Power.* New York: Quadrangle/The New York Times Book Co.: 1978.

Hargrove, Erwin C. *The Missing Link.* Washington, D.C.: Urban Institute, 1975.

Harward, Donald W. (eds.) *Crisis in Confidence.* Boston: Little, Brown, 1974.

Hougan. Jim. *Secret Agenda: Watergate, Deep Throat and the CIA.* New York: Random House, 1984.

Huntington, Samuel F. "The Democratic Distemper" *The Public Interest* 39 (Spring 1975): 10.

Jaworski, Leon. *The Right and the Power: The Prosecution of Watergate.* New York: Reader's Digest Press, 1976.

Kearns, Doris. *Lyndon Johnson and the American Dream.* New York: Harper & Row, 1976.

Kleindienst, Richard. *Justice: The Memoirs of an Attorney General.* Ottawa, IL: Jameson Books, 1985.

Kuhn, Thomas S. *The Structure of Scientific Revolution* (2nd ed., enlarged). Chicago: University of Chicago Press, 1970.

Kurland, Philip B. *Watergate and the Constitution.* Chicago: University of Chicago Press, 1978.

Kutler, Stanley I. *The Wars of Watergate: The Last Crisis of Richard Nixon.* New York: Knopf, 1990.

Lang, Gladys Engel and Kurt Lang. *The Battle for Public Opinion—the President, the press, and the polls during Watergate.* New York: Columbia University Press, 1983

LaRue, L.H. *Political Discourse—a case study of the Watergate affair.* Athens and London: The University of Georgia Press, 1988.

Liddy, Gordon G. *Will: The Autobiography of G.Gordon Liddy.* New York: St. Martin's Press. 1980.

Lipset, S.M. and E. Raab. "An Appointment with Watergate" *Commentary* 36 (Sept. 1973): 43.

Lowi, Theodore. *The End of Liberism: The Second Republic of the United States (2nd ed.).* New York: Norton, 1979.

Lukas, Anthony J. *Nightmare: The Underside of the Nixon Years.* New York: Viking Press, 1976.

Lukes, Steven. *Power: A Radical View.* London: Macmillian, 1974.

Magruder, Jeb Stuart. *An American Life.* New York: Atheneum, 1974.

Mankiewicz, Frank. *Perfectly Clear: Nixon from Whittier to Watergate.* New York: Quadrangle, 1973.

———. *U.S. vs. Richard M. Nixon: The Final Crisis.* New York: Ballantine Books, 1975.

McCord, James W. Jr. *A Piece of Tape.* Rockville, Md.: Washington Media Services, 1974.

McQuaid, Kim. *Big Business and Presidential Power: From FDR to Reagan.* New York: Morrow, 1982.

———. *The Anxious Years—America in the Vietnam-Watergate era.* New York: Basic Books, 1989.

Mendelsohn, Harold and Garrett J. O'Keefe. *The People Choose a President.* New York: Praeger, 1976.

Mintz, Morton and Jerry S. Cohen. *Power Inc.: public and private rulers and how to make them accountable.* New York: The Viking Press, 1976.

Nelson, Michael (ed.) *The Presidency and the Political System (sixth ed.).* Washington, D. C.: CQ Press, 2000.

Neustadt, Richard E. *Presidential Power—the politics of leadership from FDR to Carter.* New York: Macmillan Publishing Company, 1980.

New York Times (eds.) *The White House Transcripts.* New York: Viking Press, 1974.

Nixon, Richard M. *RN: The Memoirs of Richard Nixon* Vol.2. New York: Grosset and Dunlap, 1978.

———. *Public Papers of the Presidents of the United States: Richard Nixon* Washington, D.C.: U.S. Government Printing Office.

Osborne, John. *The Last Nixon Watch.* Washington D.C.: New Republic, 1975.

Peters, Charles. *How Washington Really Works.* Reading, MA: Addison-Wesley Publishing Co., 1980.

Philips, Kevin. *Post-Conservative America.* New York: Random House, 1982.

Popper, Karl R. *The Logic of Scientific Discovery.* London: Hutchinson Publisher, 1968.

Powers, Thomas. *The Man Who Kept the Secrets: Richard Helms and the CIA.* New York: Knopf, Pocket Books reprint, 1981.

Putnam, Robert D. *Bowling Alone: the collapse of revival of American community.* New York: Simon and Schuster, 2000..

Reedy, George. *The Twilight of the Presidency.* New York: The World Publishing Co.: 1970.

Rehniquist, William. *The Supreme Court.* New York: Morrow, 1987.

San Francisco Bay Area Kapitalistate Group "Watergate, or the Eighteenth Brumaire of Richard Nixon" *Kapitalistate* No.3 (Spring 1975): 15.

Schell, Jonathan. *The Time of Illusion: An Historical and Reflective Account of the Vietnam Era.* New York: Vintage Books, 1976.

Schlesinger, Arthur. *The Imperial Presidency.* Boston: Houghton Mifflin, 1973.

———. "How to Save the Presidency" *The Wall Street Journal*, June 10, 1973.

Schudson, Michael. *Watergate in American Memory—how we remember, forget, and reconstruct the past.* New York: Basic Books, 1992.

Skocpol, Theda. *Vision and Method in Historical Sociology.* New York: Cambridge University Press, 1984.

———. *Diminished Democracy: from membership to management in American civic life.* Norman: University of Oklahoma Press, 2003.

Skvoretz, John and Thomas J. Farato. "Power and Network Exchange: an essay toward theoretical unification" *Social Networks* 14 (1992) 325–344.

Sirica, John J. *To Set the Record Straight: The Break-in, the Tapes, the Conspirators, the Pardon.* New York: Norton, 1979.

Smith, Hedrick. *The Power Game—how Washington works.* New York: Random House, 1988.

Spear, Joseph. *President and the Press: The Nixon Legacy.* Cambridge, MA: Harvard University Press, 1984.

Sullivan, William and Bill Brown. *The Bureau: My Thirty Years in Hoover's FBI.* New York: Norton, 1979.

Sundquist, James L. *The Decline and Resurgence of Congress.* Washington D.C.: Brookings Institution, 1981.

Sussman, Barry. *The Great Cover-up.* New York: Thomas Y. Crowell, 1974.

Thompson, Fred D. *At That Point in Time: The Inside Story of the Senate Watergate Committee.* New York: Quadrangle, 1975.

Toobin, Jeffrey. *A Vast Conspiracy—the real story of the sex scandal that nearly brought down a president.* New York: Random House, 1999.

U.S. Congress, House Judiciary Committee. *Constitutional Grounds for Presidential Impeachment.* reported by the staff of the Impeachment Inquiry 93rd Congress, 2nd session. Washington, D.C.: U.S. Government Printing Office, 1974.

U.S. Congress, Senate, Select Committee. *The Final Report of the Select Committee on Presidential Campaign Activities.* Washington, D.C.: U.S. Government Printing Office, June 1974.

U.S. House of Representatives. *Hearings before the Committee on the Judiciary, 93rd Congress: Debate on Articles of Impeachment.* Washington D.C.: Government Printing Office, 1974.

Vaughan, Diane. "Theory Elaboration: the heuristics of case analysis" in *What is a Case? issues in the logic of social inquiry.* Charles C. Ragin and Howard S. Becker, eds. New York: Cambridge University Press, 1992.

Walsh, Lawrence E. *Firewall-the Iran-Contra conspiracy and cover-up.* New York and London: W.W. Norton & Company, 1997.

Weber, Max. *From Max Weber-essays in sociology.* H.H. Gerth and C. Wright Mills, eds. New York: Oxford University Press, 1958.

Wellman, Barry and S.D. Berkowitz. *Social Structures: a network approach.* Cambridge and New York: Cambridge University Press, 1988.

Wellman, Barry and Scot Wortley. "Different Strokes from Different Folks: community ties and social support" *American Journal of Sociology* Vol. 96. No.3 (Nov. 1990): 558–88.

White, Theodore. *Breach of Faith: The Fall of Richard Nixon.* New York: Atheneum, 1975.

Willer, David. "Predicting Power in Exchange Networks: a brief history and introduction to the issues" *Social Networks* 14 (1992): 187–211.

Woodward, Bob and Scott Armstrong. *The Brethren: Inside the Supreme Court.* New York: Simon & Schuster, 1979.

Woodward, Bob and Carl Bernstein. *The Final Days.* New York: Simon & Schuster, 1976.

Index

abuse of power, 11, 12, 105, 106, 109, 117
Administrative Practice Subcommittee, 34, 38
AFL-CIO, 11, 85, 108
Agnew, Spiro, 119, 120
Albert, Carl, 27, 87, 88
Anderson, John, 100, 106, 113
Anti-Vietnam War movement, 2
April 30th explosion, 13, 61, 71, 73, 80
Arends, Leslie, 107
arrogance of power, 2, 11, 13, 18

Baker, Howard, 39–42, 54, 58–59, 74, 82, 92
Bay Area Kapitalistate Group, 125–26
Bennett, Wallace, 119
Berstein, Carl, 21, 43, 45, 63, 79, 95
Boschwitz, Rudy, 86
Break-in, 13; exposure of, 16, 20–21, 23, 33–34, 38, 43, 45, 52, 55, 60, 63, 118; frame of, 76, 79–80, 82, 91–91, 105; incident of, 2
Brennan, William, 112
Brock, Bill, 119
Buchanan, Patrick, 94
Buckley, James, 60, 86
Burger, Warren, 110–12
Burger Court, the, 110

Burns, Arthur, 23
Bush, George, 95, 100, 108
Butler, Caldwell, 108
Byrd, Robert, 45, 67

checks and balances, 7, 78, 128
Chern, Vicky, 55
Chomsky, Noam, 126–27
Church, Frank, 9
CIA, 17–19, 63, 105
Civil Rights movement, 2
Clinton, Bill, 6–7, 114–15
Cohen, Jerry S., 124–25
Cohen, William, 97–98, 107, 109
collective power dynamics. *See* Washington collective power dynamics
collective unconsciousness, 68
Colson, Charles, 11, 16, 73, 110
Committee to Re-Elect the President (CREEP), 2, 4, 16, 18–23, 97; as target of investigations, 33, 42, 50, 52, 63
Compbell, Donald, 20
Conable, Barber, 94–95, 100
Connally, John, 23–24, 93
conservative perspective, 12, 123–24
Cook, Marlow, 59
Cotton, Norris, 60, 119

cover-up, 3; exposure of, 43–46, 50, 52–56, 60, 65, 66; frame of, 76, 79–80, 82, 91–92, 109; incident of, 19, 21–25, 27
Cox, Archibald, 21, 62–64, 71, 80, 84, 93
Cranston, Alan, 64
critical left perspective, 126–27

Dash, Sam, 41–43, 51–52, 55, 57; role in Ervin Committee public hearings, 71, 73–74, 81–82, 84, 91–92
Dean, John, 1, 3, 11, 60, 61, 63, 81, 109; Defection, 44–46, 53–57, 59, 65–66; role in cover-up, 16, 17, 19, 20, 21, 23–24, 42
Democratic Party, 3, 6, 22, 109
Dent, Harry, 110
DiMaggio, Paul, 129–30
Doar, John, 99, 108
Dole, Bob, 6, 21
Dominick, Peter, 93
Douglas, William O., 111–12
Doyle, James, 64

Eastland, James O., 34–35
Ehrlichman, John, 55–57, 61, 63, 73, 82, 111; role in Watergate, 4, 9, 11, 18, 19, 35
Eisenhower, Julie Nixon, 108
Ellsberg, Daniel, 19
embeddedness, social, 127, 129
enemies list, 11
Ervin, Sam, 13, 33–34, 37. *See also* Ervin Committee
Ervin Committee, 13, 17, 21, 27, 29, 65, 67; creation of, 35, 38, 39, 40; end of public hearings, 91, 92; final report, 105; investigation, 42, 43, 46, 51, 52, 54–58; public hearings, 68, 71, 74, 75, 77, 79, 81–83, 112
executive privilege, 42, 56, 109, 111
expletive deleted, 94

FBI, 16–19, 39, 44–45, 63, 85, 98, 105
Fish, Hamilton, 100–101, 108

Flowers, Walter, 109
Ford, Gerald R., 21, 23, 26, 108, 120
Fortas, Abe, 110
Fragile Coalition, 106–7, 113
Fulbright, William J., 9, 59

Gamson, William, 127, 135
Gemstone file, 17
genuine communication, 72, 77
Glanzer, Seymour, 20
Glaser, Barney, 146, 147
Goldwater, Berry, 4–5, 39; role in uncoupling, 60–61, 64–66, 93–94, 98, 100, 118–20
Goldwater, Berry, Jr., 65
GOP. *See* Republican Party
Graham, Billy, 11
Granovetter, Mark, 137
Gray, Pat, 17, 18, 20, 58, 61. *See also* Gray Hearings
Gray Hearings, 44–46, 51, 53, 55. *See also* Gray, Pat
Gray-McMord-Sirica Shocks, 10
Great Society, the, 3
Griffin, Robert, 119
Gurney, Edward, 40–41, 59

Haig, Alexander, 119
Haldman, Bob, 55–57, 61, 63, 73, 82, 118; role in Watergate, 10–11, 17–19, 23, 37–38
Hall, Leonard, 46
Harlow, Bryce, 94
Harmony, Sally, 55
Heckler, Margaret, 26
Helms, Jesse, 35, 39
Helms, Richard, 17–18, 63
Hoover, Edgar J., 19, 25, 44, 45
House Banking and Currency Committee. *See* Patman Committee
House Judiciary Committee, 88–89, 102, 106–9, 112–19
House Republican Policy Conference, 95, 113
Humphrey, Hubert, 34, 92

Hunt, Howard, 2, 17, 19–21, 50, 52
Huntington, Samuel, 124
Huston Plan, 105
Hutchinson, Edward, 88

Impeachment, 65, 67–68, 81, 85–88, 95–102; final proceedings, 105–21, 127
Impoundment, 10
interpersonal connections. *See* interpersonal network
interpersonal network, 36, 40, 47–48, 107, 128–29; role in Watergate, 5–7, 13, 24, 27
interpersonal power dynamics, 13, 15, 16, 22, 26, 45, 77
Iran-Contra Affair, 6
Internal Revue Service (IRS), 11, 105–6

Javits, Jacob, 86, 119
Jaworski, Leon, 87, 99, 111–12
Johnson, Lyndon, 1, 3–4, 23, 64, 110, 118
Jonas, Charles, 37
Justice, Department of, 20–22, 24, 26, 84; institutional function of, 51–53, 56, 61, 63

Kenney, Edward, 9, 11, 34, 38, 40, 64
Kissinger, Henry, 9, 102
Kleindienst, Richard, 20, 21, 42, 61, 62
Kuhn, Thomas, 143

Laird, Melvin, 95
leftist view, 13, 125–27
Lenzner, Terry, 71
Lewinsky, Monica, 7, 115
liberal perspective, 12, 124–25
Liddy, Gordon G., 2, 16–21, 24, 33, 50, 53, 85
Lincoln, Abraham, 116
Lipset, S.M., 123–24
Louch, Hugh, 129–30
Lugar, Richard, 6

MacGregor, Clark, 21
Magruder, Jeb, 4, 16, 21–22, 42, 53–57, 63
Mann, James, 106, 108–9
Mansfield, Mike, 13, 33–35, 38, 40, 43
Mansfield Amendment, 4
Mansfield-Ervin Alliance, 38–40
Marumoto, William, 91
mass society, 72
Maximum John, 48, 50
McCloskey, Paul, 67
McCord, James, 2, 20, 50, 52–54
McGovern, George, 21–22, 28, 30, 50, 59, 61, 64, 106
Meany, George, 85
Michel, Robert, 100
Milliken, William, 86
Mintz, Morton, 124–25
Mitchell, John, 4, 16–17, 20–25, 54–56, 67, 111
Mondale, Walter, 11
Muskie, Edmund, 11, 34, 59

national collective power dynamics, 85–87, 90, 137
Neal, James F., 64
Neo-Progressivism, 136–38
New American Majority, 9
New Minority, 9
Nixon, Richard: fighting the Washington collective power, 34–48; final stage of resignation, 105–20; in the eyes of the public, 75–77; in theory, 123–28, 131; interpersonal relationship in Washington in general, 1, 3–5, 7, 9–13; involvement in cover-up, 14–19, 22–23, 26–28, 30; on death-bed politically, 56–68; under the pressure of uncoupling, 79–79–88, 90–102

obstruction of justice, 11, 21, 23, 56, 63, 99; impeachment proceedings, 106, 115, 117, 119
O'Brien, Francis, 113

O'Brien, Larry, 11, 22–23
O'Connor, James O., 125–26
Odle, Robert, 16

Panarites, Sylvia, 55
Parkinson, Kenneth, 24
Patman, Wright, 23–24, 28, 39, 43, 52. *See also* Patman Committee
Patman Committee (House Banking and Currency Committee), 23–27
Petersen, Henry, 20, 23–24, 52, 56, 61
Plumbers (Special Investigative Unit), 2, 11, 56, 63, 105
Political Affairs, Office of, 110
Popper, Karl, 143
Price, Ray, 94
Proxmire, William, 9, 23
Public Liaison, Office of, 110
Putman, Robert, D., 137

Raab, E., 123–24
radical left, 125–26
Railsback, Tom, 86, 100, 108–9
Reagan, Ronald, 5–6, 97
Rebozo Fund, 92
Rehnquist, William, 111
Reisner, Robert, 55
Republican National Committee (RNC), 4, 46, 95
Republican Party, 3–4, 6, 59–60, 66–67, 108, 118, 120; uncoupling, 90, 94, 96, 98, 100
Responsiveness Program, 91, 105
Rhodes, John, 95, 98, 100–101, 118, 120
Richardson, Elliot, 62, 63, 84, 108
Rockefeller, Nelson, 24, 25, 63, 97, 108
Rodino, Peter, 88, 107, 112
Rogers, William, 46–47
Roosevelt, Franklin D., 3–4
Ruckelshaus, William, 84
rule of law, 116
Russell, Richard, 36

Sampson, Arthur, 79
Saturday Night Massacre, 13, 78–80, 87, 90–91, 93–94, 120
Schorr, Daniel, 84
Scott, Hugh, 39, 59, 79, 95, 118–20
Senate Resolution 60, 40
Senate Select Committee. *See* Ervin Committee
Senate Watergate Committee. *See* Ervin Committee
separation of powers, 7, 127, 129
Silbert, Earl, 20–22, 50, 54, 56–57, 63
Silent Majority. *See* New American Majority
Sirica, John, 46–48, 51–53, 57, 109
Skocpol, Theda, 137
socially constructed power dynamics. *See* Washington collective power dynamics
Special Investigative Unit. *See* Plumbers
Special Prosecutor, 63, 81, 85, 87, 99
Speight, Jack, 86
St. Clair, 111–12
Stans, Maurice, 23–24, 67
Stennis Compromise, 84–85
stone-walling, 3, 108, 118
Strauss, Anselm L., 146, 147
Strength of weak ties, 137–38
Super-Cabinet officers, 9, 10
Supreme Court, 7, 63, 99, 101–2, 109–12

Teapot Dome, 28, 60–61
theory elaboration, 142–44
third-rate burglary, 2, 46
Thompson, Fred, 41, 57, 81, 92
Thornton, Ray, 86, 109
Timmons, Bill, 23
Titus, Harold, 20
Tower, John, 39, 60, 119

ultra-right, 12
uncoupling, 13, 41, 59, 83, 90, 93–94, 97, 109

Vaughan, Diane, 143
Vietnam War, 4, 77

Washington collective power dynamics, 11, 13, 22, 27, 29, 30; final result of, 106–10, 112–15, 117–19, 121; formation of, 33–34, 36–37, 39, 40–44, 46, 48; strength of, 51–52, 54–56, 58–59, 61–64, 67–68; theoretical discussion of, 128–30; weakness of, 72–73, 75, 77, 79–81, 83–85, 87, 90–92, 94–96, 99–100, 102
Washington iron triangle, 10
Washington nervous system, 83
Washington Post, 19, 21, 28, 86, 93, 111

Watergate burglars (Watergate Seven), 42, 50, 52
Waters, Vernon, 17–18, 63
Wayne, John, 11
Weber, Max, 128
webs of interpersonal ties. *See* interpersonal networks
Weicker, Lowell, 40–41, 58, 82, 92
White House Taping System, 80–81
Wiggins, Charles, 118
Woodward, Bob, 21, 34, 38, 43, 45, 55, 63, 79, 95

Yom Kippur War, 84

Ziegler, Ronald L., 2, 55, 61, 85